First published by UPA Books, 2022
An initiative of United Publishers of Armidale, www.unitedpublishersofarmidale.net
UPA Books is a collaboration between two independent publishing houses:
Christmas Press & Little Pink Dog Books

In association with the New England Writers' Centre, www.newc.org.au

Inside Story: the wonderful world of writing, illustrating and publishing children's books

First published by UPA Books, 2022
An initiative of United Publishers of Armidale, www.unitedpublishersofarmidale.net

In association with the New England Writers' Centre, www.newc.org.au
Compiled by Sophie Masson, Kathy Creamer, Beattie Alvarez and Peter Creamer
Edited by Jen Scanlan and Sharnee Rawson
Designed by Rae Ainsworth

ISBN 978-0-64881545-7

A catalogue record for this
book is available from the
National Library of Australia

The Inside Story project is supported by the NSW Government through Create NSW.

INSIDE STORY:

the wonderful world of writing, illustrating and publishing children's books

Compiled by

Sophie Masson, Kathy Creamer, Beattie Alvarez and Peter Creamer

Edited by Jen Scanlan and Sharnee Rawson. Designed by Rae Ainsworth

For Grace, Juliet, Flynn & Eli – who each,
in their own creative ways, artistically or
technologically, are next generation future leaders.

FOREWORD

The more that you read, the more things you will know. The more that you learn, the more places you'll go. — **Dr Seuss, *I Can Read With My Eyes Shut***

Inside Story equips you to read, know, learn and travel along the varied pathways towards publication. Taking you into the heart of children's writing, illustrating and publishing, it mines the generosity of some of the best and brightest authors, illustrators, publishers, agents, designers and marketers.

Discover the 'nuts and bolts' of publication, priceless wisdom and the professional journey. The great insights of contributors will become the hook for many in creating their own children's books. The acknowledgements list the many contributors who provided invaluable advice about children's books, from literary agent Alexandra Adsett to author Michelle Worthington. These contributors are the who's who of children's book publishing.

'Children love discovery, so they will be happy to learn!' (Ursula Dubosarsky Australian Laureate 2020–2021). So will the readers of this invaluable resource.

While *Inside Story* shows the great challenges of creating books, it also shows that support for each other within the industry is a foundation stone that makes the creation of children's books such a wonderful world.

Susanne Gervay OAM
Regional Advisor
The Society of Children's Book Writers and Illustrators, Australia East and New Zealand.

WRITING

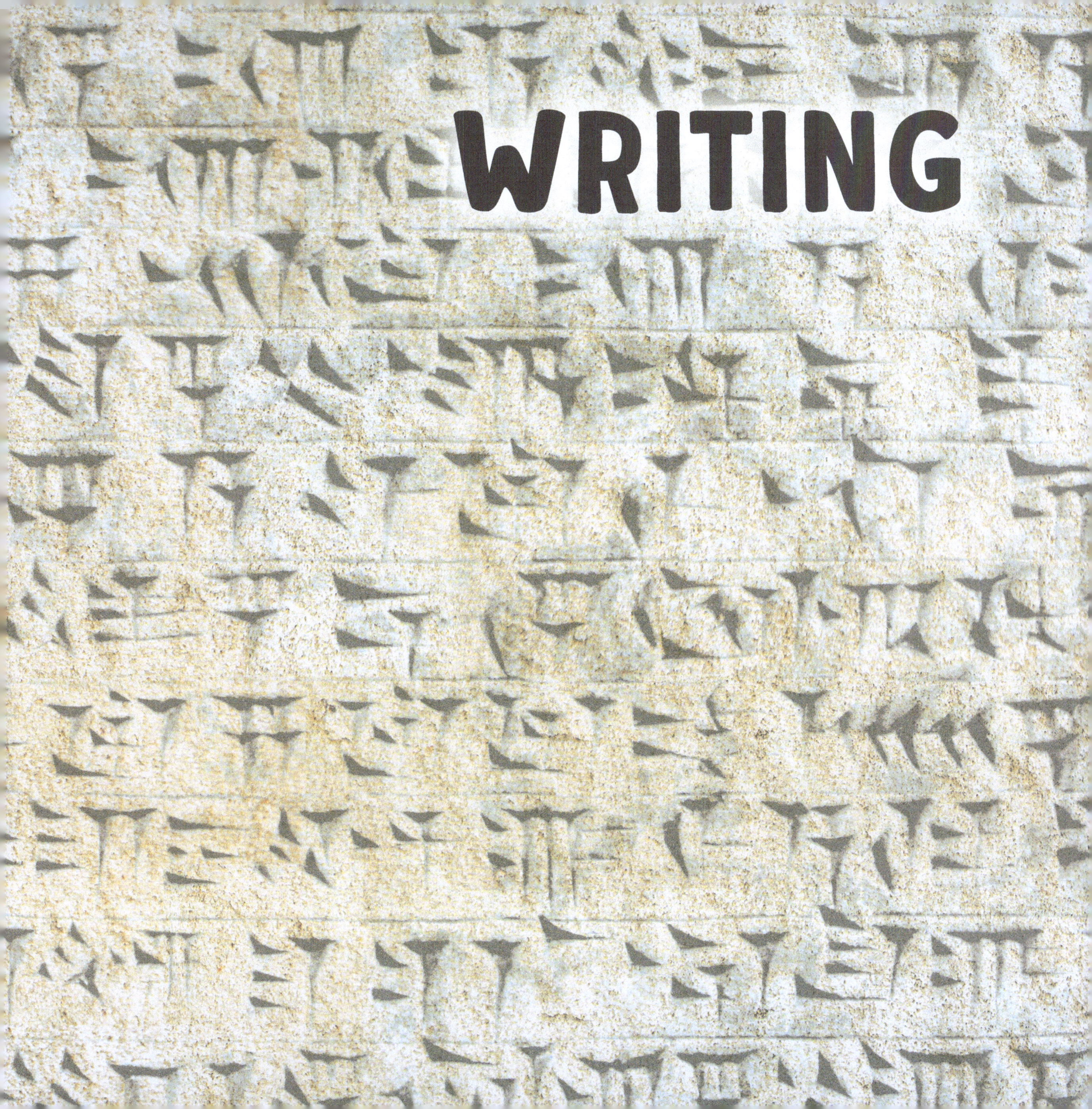

PICTURE BOOK TEXTS

WHAT IS A PICTURE BOOK? SIMPLY PUT, IT IS A UNIQUE COLLABORATION BETWEEN THE CREATIVITY OF AN AUTHOR AND THE CREATIVITY OF AN ILLUSTRATOR.

OCCASIONALLY, THOSE TWO THINGS EXIST IN ONE PERSON: THE AUTHOR-ILLUSTRATOR, OR AS WE MIGHT CALL THEM, THE 'AUTHORSTRATOR.'

Authorstrators not only create picture books with text and illustration but also wordless picture books where the illustrations tell the entire story. More often than not, though, the author and the illustrator are two individual people. In a few cases, they may know each other personally, but usually, they do not. The publisher brings them together, along with the editor and designer who will play an important part in helping the picture book to its full potential.

In the contemporary publishing landscape, picture books are generally full-colour productions between 24 and 32 pages long, and between 100 and 500 words in length. (In *Inside Story*, we use the term 'illustrated storybooks' for individual picture books that have longer texts, up to 2,000 words).

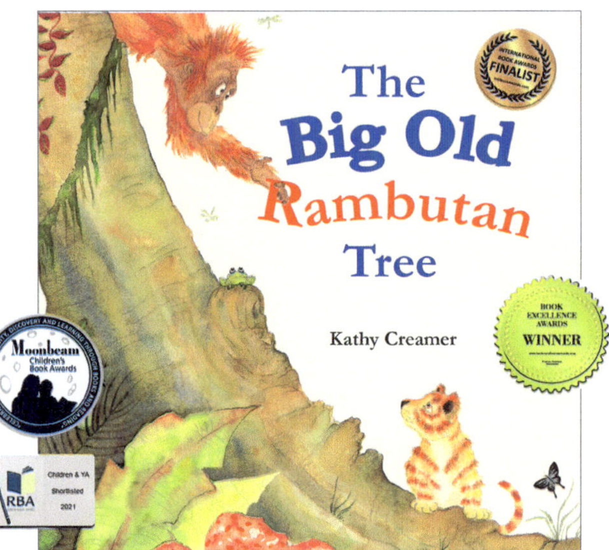

The age range at which picture books are usually aimed varies between babyhood to mid-primary school (aged 0 to 10 years), with the occasional older picture book published.

The majority of picture books begin with an author's text, acquired by a publisher and then sent by them to an illustrator. As they are so often the building block of a picture book, texts are vitally important.

Sometimes, people seem to be under the impression that because of their short length, picture book texts are 'easy' to write. Nothing could be further from the truth!

CHECK OUT

Four classic Australian picture books:

There's a Hippopotamus on Our Roof Eating Cake (first published 1980) by Hazel Edwards and Deborah Niland, Hodder and Stoughton; *Possum Magic* (first published 1983) by Mem Fox and Julie Vivas, Omnibus Books; *The Bunyip of Berkeley's Creek* (first published 1973) by Jenny Wagner and Ron Brooks, Viking; *There's a Sea in My Bedroom* (first published 1984) by Margaret Wild and Jane Tanner, Viking.

The 1970s and 1980s in Australia saw an explosion of picture book talent, and these beloved classics from that time have been part of many people's childhoods over the decades they have been continuously in print.

Hazel Edwards writes about why her text for *There's a Hippopotamus on Our Roof Eating Cake* has struck such an enduring chord with readers over the generations:

The reassurance of a BIG imaginary friend who has all the answers is relevant for apprehensive young children. It was inspired by a real 4 year old, but it's a universal experience. It reads aloud well for parents (especially beaut Dads doing funny voices) and there's humour with the absurdity of cake being eaten by a hippo.

A small selection of recent Australian picture books:

All of the Factors of Why I Love Tractors (2019) by Davina Bell and Jenny Lovlie, Little Hare; *The World's Worst Pirate* (2017) by Michelle Worthington and Katrin Dreiling, Little Pink Dog Books; *One Step at a Time* (2015) by Jane Jolly and Sally Heinrich, MidnightSun Publishing; *Mad Magpie* (2016) written and illustrated by Gregg Dreise, Magabala Books; *Aunty's Wedding* (2020) by Miranda Tapsell, Joshua Tyler and Samantha Fry, Allen & Unwin; *Go to Sleep, Jessie* (2014) by Libby Gleeson and Freya Blackwood, Little Hare; *Where Happiness Hides* (2020) by Anthony Bertini and Jennifer Goldsmith, Dirt Lane Press; *Night Lights* (2021) by Inda Ahmad Zahri and Lesley McGee, Little Pink Dog Books; *The Very Noisy Baby* (2017) written and illustrated by Alison Lester, Affirm Press; *My Friend Fred* (2020) by Frances Watts and A.Yi, Allen & Unwin; *The March of the Ants* (2021) by Ursula Dubosarsky and Tohby Riddle, Book Trail Press; *Good Question* (2020) by Sue Whiting and Annie White, Walker Books.

GENERAL WRITING TIPS

- The inspiration for a picture book can come from just as many places as for longer works. But as you don't have as many words to explore that idea, you have to be very choosy about the words you do use! Be prepared to craft and edit a great deal.
- Story is important in picture book texts, even if that story is very simple and the timeline is short (e.g. bedtime). The beginning, middle and ending should form a satisfying story arc.
- A twist or surprise at the end can be good, but you shouldn't force a twist; you just need to find a satisfying ending.
- Don't be hung up on 'your' vision of the illustrations; the illustrator needs as much creative freedom as you had in creating your text. However, it's useful to have a sense of the potential visual atmosphere of your work, as publishers will often ask if you have a vision, even if it is sketchy.
- Most importantly, READ! Get your hands on as many picture books as you can – have a look at the books we've listed, but don't limit yourself to that, of course!

This selection of 12 recent picture books represents a wide range of stories and creators – from emerging to established. However, they were also chosen to illustrate the fact that, in recent years, small and medium independent publishers have built a strong place within children's book publishing in Australia, enhancing publication opportunities for authors and illustrators.

Advice from writers

Michelle Worthington's advice for aspiring authors of picture books:

Aspiring authors who are thinking they would like to write for children should start by reading a bunch of picture books that have been published in the last five years. You need to create stories that today's children will enjoy by finding the right topic, language and pace, but also using their unique voice to engage the reader in a way that screens can't. Lots of ideas could lead to an endearing story, but nothing will become published unless you write it. Sharing your story with the world might just make it a better place.

The spark of a text – Sophie Masson on inspiration:

A similar inspiration doesn't mean the same writing process when it comes to a picture book text. For example, although both *The Snowman's Wish* (Dirt Lane Press) and *There's a Tiger Out There* (Little Hare) started with images from dreams, the writing process for each was very different. With *There's a Tiger Out There*, my first draft had the dream tiger turning into a real-life cat. A few drafts later, working with my editors and seeing illustrator Ruth Waters' gorgeous samples, the story had completely changed so that the closeness and imaginative power of the two siblings in the story were central, with the tiger remaining elusive. With *The Snowman's Wish*, the image in the dream created such a powerful story in my mind that I pretty much wrote it down as soon as I woke up. It hardly changed at all during the editing process, just a word or two to better accommodate illustrator Ronak Taher's brilliant conjuring of the visual world of the text. Similarly, both *See Monkey* and *A House of Mud* (both Little Pink Dog Books) come from real-life family experiences, but *See Monkey* was written briskly in one day over three handwritten drafts, while *A House of Mud* took me years to get right before I sent it to a publisher. (In each case, of course, they found the perfect illustrators – respectively, Kathy Creamer and Katrina Fisher). So, the moral of the tale is every text is different, and there's no set way for the process to happen!

Picture books are short. Keep the text spare, focusing on the action and omitting anything better expressed by illustration. And the text needs rhythm so read it aloud to see if it flows. **— Libby Gleeson**

Read lots of poetry (aloud!) and write poetry too. Not simply for the sense of rhyme that is found in many children's poems, but to develop a feel for the rhythm, spare prose and word choice, all of which are vital in picture book writing. In a nutshell, a picture book is like a short story in poetry form.
— Janeen Brian

P4/5

I'm a dirty dinosaur

with a dirty tum.

I sprinkle it with mud –

~~and~~ or I tap it like a drum.

I wobble it like jelly

Modelling is an important tool for a beginner picture book writer. Find a picture book you love, read it aloud, write it out by hand, see how the words flow, study the structure, the language and the rhythm. Now write a story using what you've learned. Do this again and again and again. **— Lesley Gibbes**

roar like a lion,

Advice from publishers and agents

What publishers look for in picture books:

We look for interesting stories that when read out loud have rhythm and lively language. They have to be visual, with the words leaving space for the illustrator to share the narrative with visual action. We look for stories that will entertain and enthral children, make them laugh, cry, comfort them and give them a positive 'take-away' message. **— Kathy Creamer, publisher, Little Pink Dog Books**

To creators of picture books and books for our youngest readers, I implore you to think about the grown-up on the other end of your work reading and exploring the book with a child ... night after night after night! The most cherished books in the home library are ones that grown-ups are happy to read over and over again. Don't forget the grown-up! **— Tash Besliev, publisher, Children's Books, Affirm Press**

Publishing a picture book is a big decision – the production costs are high, finding the right illustrator can be a drawn-out process, and because the area is so competitive, we must feel confident that the story will stand the test of time. So, a picture book must be heartbreakingly beautiful, have a breathtakingly ingenious twist or a powerful and universal message – or ideally, all three – for me to want to take it on. **— Eva Mills, publishing director, Books for Children and Young Adults, Allen & Unwin**

Picture books are the product of a creative partnership between a writer and an illustrator. If you're the writer, remember to respect that the illustrator is your collaborator, your equal, not someone doing a job for you (try to banish the phrase 'my illustrator' from your life). The illustrator is the visual expert, so let them bring their skills to the project: you have created a story through your words and now it's up to them to create a visual narrative. **— Chren Byng, head of Australian Children's Publishing, HarperCollins Australia**

Don't assume because there are fewer words in a picture book text that they are easier to write! A full-length novel of 90,000 words can afford to have a few imperfect ones; a 350-word picture book text needs every single word to be the right one. Remember too that if you are writing rhyming text, the lines must scan as well as rhyme, and be aware that rhyming texts are much more difficult to place in translation territories, so publishers tend to shy away from them unless they are brilliant. **— Fiona Inglis, managing director, Curtis Brown literary agency**

An illustrator's view

The text is my cue. I interpret the story, as I understand it. I imagine the settings, characters and props. I don't like being given extra visual suggestions. It puts blinkers on my imagination. The best texts are spare and often leave much of the emotional story content to be suggested visually. **— Ann James, illustrator and co-director of Books Illustrated.**

ILLUSTRATED STORYBOOKS

ILLUSTRATED STORYBOOKS ARE SIMILAR TO PICTURE BOOKS BUT LONGER IN LENGTH – BOTH IN PAGE COUNT AND WORD COUNT.

The average (and this varies greatly) picture book is from 100 to 500 words. Illustrated storybooks are normally upwards of 1,000 words. They can be read to younger children who enjoy the story and the pictures or read by older children. They can have one long story or two short stories – or more – within one volume.

Illustrations can be full colour or a mix of colour and black and white images. As with all illustrations, the styles vary depending on the story and the targeted age of the reader. The illustrations may also be more detailed than picture book illustrations. They are there to enhance the text, not replace it, as in the case of some picture books.

An illustrated storybook manuscript should be able to be read and understood without illustrations, meaning that you don't need them to tell you what's going on, although the illustrations of a finished storybook will help the reader to visualise the story.

In some ways, that makes writing the text easier, but you still need to have a good story! It needs to have a beginning, middle and ending. It needs to be exciting, page turning AND easy to read aloud. Language is important, of course. You need to keep in mind that some readers will still be in the early stages of reading; however, there's more leeway in your language and storyline choices. You can have more complex ideas and language in illustrated storybooks – just look at any collection of fairytales. Some of the storylines in fairytales are quite mature for young readers but they have stood the test of time. Consider grandmothers being eaten by wolves, as in *Red Riding Hood*, beasts keeping young girls hostage, as in *Beauty and the Beast*, and jealous witches putting teenagers in comas, as in *Snow White.*

GENERAL WRITING TIPS

- Be mindful of reading age, but don't dumb the text down. This is a chance for the reader or listener to learn new words and ideas.
- Make your characters engaging – the good and the bad.
- This is your chance to tell a full story – don't hold back!
- Edit!
- Read, read, read – of course! Check out our selections below but don't limit yourself to them.

Three illustrated storybooks of fairy tale retellings from Christmas Press:

Two Selkie Stories from Scotland (2014) by Kate Forsyth and Fiona McDonald; *Two Tales of Brothers from Ancient Mesopotamia* (2016) by John Heffernan and Kate Durack; *Two Enchanted Tales from Old China* (2018) by Gabrielle Wang and David Allan. You can also check out other Christmas Press illustrated storybooks in the *Two Tales* series at https://christmaspresspicturebooks.com/two-tales-series/.

A small selection of illustrated storybooks from other publishers:

Shirley Barber's *Wonderland Treasury* and Shirley Barber's *Fairyland Treasury* (both 2018) written and illustrated by Shirley Barber, Brolly Books; *The Tales of Mrs Mancini* (2016) and also *The Fairy Dancers* (2015) both by Natalie Jane Prior and Cheryl Orsin, HarperCollins; *The Cleo Stories* (2014–2015) by Libby Gleeson and Freya Blackwood, Allen & Unwin; *Introducing D'Lila Rue* (2021) by Nette Hilton and Anne Yi, Walker Books; Wombat, *Mudlark and Other Stories* (2019) by Helen Milroy, Fremantle Press.

Advice from writers

I love the chance to combine the charm and lure of the original story with your own special take. That way you are part of the traditional tale, and yet you reach beyond it. *Two Tales of Brothers from Ancient Mesopotamia* is a truly ancient story, but in telling it, I have also tried to make it an allegory of modern 'Mesopotamia.'
— John Heffernan

Every single sentence, every single scene, must have some clear purpose in a story for children. And I think it's a mistake to always choose the simplest, most basic words. Children love language. Their minds are hungry for it. If the language of a story is sinuous and surprising, the child will be enchanted and curious to know more. The rhythm of the words become an irresistible current that sweeps them away to new lands and new adventures. **— Kate Forsyth**

Anthony Sevil's first book, *Hector and his Highland Dancers*, an illustrated storybook with illustrator Amy Calautti, was published in 2020 by Little Pink Dog Books and shortlisted in the 2020 Speech Pathology Australia Book of the Year Awards. He talks about his journey as a first-time author:

Hector and his Highland Dancers came at the end of a long and spasmodic writing journey. Now, with my first book out at the age of 75, it feels like it's the beginning! Over the years, I had some publication success with non-fiction stories but not fiction. Then, in 2011, out of frustration, I undertook a creative writing course with Writing NSW. That proved a turning point. Because of it, I developed a bush character for a humorous crime story, which ended up winning me an award in the 2014 New England Thunderbolt Crime Writing Prize (an annual national competition run by the New England Writers' Centre). In 2015, that same story was published in a Melbourne Books' anthology. This gave me more confidence, and I started to write more regularly and with a greater understanding of what works.

I've always liked having chickens around and have been impressed and somewhat amused at the dedication of chicken breeders and their show birds. So, I asked myself – what if a breeder's prized show bird could never win a competition due to an unfortunate habit?

What could the guy do with his pride and joy? And then came the light bulb moment. It could become a Highland dancer, of course! That was how the character of Hector came about. My mother was always glued to the Edinburgh Tattoo so that had to be the grand finale for the chicken dancers. I was extraordinarily lucky to find a publisher who appreciated my writing and my rather wacky sense of humour! Since then, my confidence as a writer has increased, and I am working on more picture book stories. Becoming a published picture book author has changed my life. So, to anyone out there who hopes to be published: it's never too late!

FICTION ANTHOLOGIES

ANTHOLOGIES IN THIS INSTANCE MEAN A COLLECTION OF STORIES, GENERALLY SHORT, BY A NUMBER OF AUTHORS, WHICH ARE BROUGHT TOGETHER BY A COMPILER FOR PUBLICATION IN A SINGLE BOOK. (POETRY ANTHOLOGIES ARE COVERED IN 'POETRY AND VERSE NOVELS' ON PAGE 25).

Sometimes authors will be invited to contribute a story, and sometimes there's an open call for submissions – meaning that anyone can submit a story, but not all will be chosen. There will always be a central theme. For instance, the Christmas Press anthology *A Miniature Christmas* (2018) had stories based around little things. There were stories about mice under the floorboards, elves that communicated by jumping on computer keyboards and flower fairies trying hard to create the perfect Christmas. As this publisher only brings out anthologies at Christmas time, they need to put a twist on the overall theme of Christmas; otherwise, it gets boring very quickly.

Anthologies from other publishers may not be arranged around a seasonally defined theme or an age group. Writing to a theme can be hard. How do you know what other people have written or submitted? Have you met the brief properly? The Christmas Press anthologies generally have a word limit of 2000 words per story and an age range of 6 to 10 year olds, but of course, these will vary from publisher to publisher.

How does the compiler choose the stories? Well, they pick the ones that best match the theme, but there's more to it than that. The stories have to be well written, engaging and interesting.

Sometimes a few similar stories will tick all those boxes. It then comes down to the personal taste of the compiler, and there's not a whole lot you can do about it. A lot of coffee and conversations with team members play a big part in it too.

So far, they've published *Once Upon a Christmas*, which was their first and had a general Christmas theme, *Three Dragons for Christmas*, *A Toy Christmas*, *A Christmas Menagerie*, *A Miniature Christmas* and *A Christmas Cornucopia* (all about food).

One idea that was rejected was 'A Ghostly Christmas' over fears that it might be too scary. Another possibility was 'A Mystery Christmas', but there's been discussion that too many submissions might revolve around missing presents!

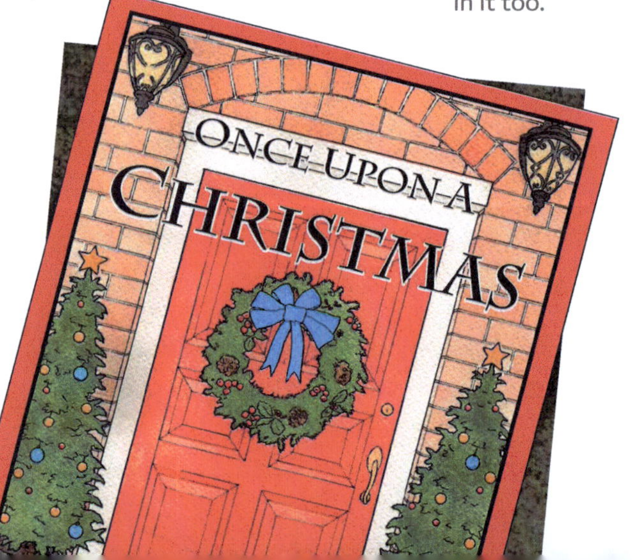

CHECK OUT

An additional selection of fiction anthologies:

Stories for Five Year Olds (2012), *Stories for Six Year Olds* (2012), *Stories for Seven Year Olds* (2014) and *Stories for Eight Year Olds* (2012), all edited by Linsay Knight, Random House Australia; *Funny Bones* (2019) edited by Oliver Phommavanh, Kate Temple and Jol Temple, Allen & Unwin; *Kids' Night In* (2003) edited by Nick Earls and *Kids' Night In 2* (2005) edited by Jessica Adams, both published by Penguin.

TIPS FROM A COMPILER

- Read the brief and follow it. That's one of the golden rules if you don't want to get an immediate rejection.
- Try to come up with something different. Think outside the box. We know that there's nothing new under the sun, but you can put your twist on things.
- Read your story aloud, as it's a book of stories for children, to see if it works.
- Make sure you've given it an edit and a proofread, preferably with a professional editor. One way to make sure that a compiler won't read the whole story is to have spelling mistakes and misused punctuation.
- READ. A lot! The more you read, the more you'll know what's already out there. Reading stories in the theme and age range for the anthology will also help.
- Enjoy what you write. Don't write something just to get published. Write something because you love writing and have a story to tell.

Advice from writers

What I love about writing short stories for kids is that the structure has to be clean and pure. It's the best exercise in plotting there is. And I love reconnecting with the perspectives that children have: the importance of things like insects, frogs and the colour of the sky. That's why writing for a themed anthology is both a challenge and a relief. A challenge, because you must be creative around a topic you previously might not have thought about. A relief, as this allows you to brutally reject ideas you'd otherwise play with for weeks. — **Anna Bell**

I love writing for themed anthologies. Having a theme will often get me writing about something that I wouldn't otherwise have thought to try. My first thought, when asked to contribute to *A Miniature Christmas*, was decorations, but I wanted to find an unusual way of writing about them. So, I wrote about a fairy trap that was disguised as a decoration. Also, I will often pepper my fiction with bits of real life. It helps me anchor even the most bizarre and fantastical stories, hopefully making them relatable. The events of 'Pudding Prize' (*A Toy Christmas*), for example, are completely fictitious, but they draw upon my Russian heritage, my fascination with traditions and my love of cooking. — **George Ivanoff**

GRAPHIC NOVELS

GRAPHIC NOVELS FOR CHILDREN, SOMETIMES CALLED COMIC BOOKS, HAVE A LONG HISTORY IN COUNTRIES SUCH AS FRANCE, JAPAN AND THE US, WITH THE GENRE FLOURISHING THERE FROM THE LATE NINETEENTH TO EARLY TWENTIETH CENTURY.

Many graphic novels are popular with both home markets and international audiences. These include the *bandes dessinées* (BDs) or 'drawn strips' books of France, such as the *Tintin* and *Asterix* series, the manga (a word derived from 'whimsical pictures') books of Japan, such as *Astro Boy*, and the comics of the USA, including *Popeye* and *Mickey Mouse* as well as the superhero comics. In those countries, especially France and Japan, the genre is highly regarded.

However, until fairly recently in Australia (and the UK), graphic novels or comic books were often regarded as lesser quality than other forms of fiction. Small niche publishers were producing graphic novels but mostly these were for adults. It wasn't until the 1990s that children's books publishers started to take an interest in the genre, with such titles as Norman Jorgensen and Allan Langoulant's *Ashe of the Outback* (1992) but even then only a few were published.

In the 2000s, things started to change, with much of that change being directly attributable to recognition of the extraordinary work of Shaun Tan. Today, you can find many graphic novels for children, as well as those books that use a mix of graphic novel and classic narrative techniques. Some non-fiction also uses graphic novel elements and techniques.

Graphic novels can be in colour or black and white, and they cover a range of stories from fantasy to humour, realism to mystery and much more. Many graphic novels may also cross over into picture books, such as Shaun Tan's *The Lost Thing* (2000), which could be seen either as a graphic novel or as a picture book.

Graphic novels are often created by authorstrators such as Shaun Tan, whose working notebooks you can see on this page. Some graphic novels feature an author and illustrator team. In that case, it works rather like a picture book, with the author being the originator of the story, then the publisher bringing in an illustrator to create the visual world.

CHECK OUT

A small selection of graphic novels, from the mid-2000s to now:

The Arrival (2006) and *Cicada* (2018) by Shaun Tan, Hachette Australia; *Ubby's Underdogs* series (2011–2019) by Brenton McKenna, Magabala Books; *Bad Guys* series (2015–2021) by Aaron Blabey, Scholastic; *The Nelly Gang* (2013) by Stephen Axelsen, Walker Books; *Fly on the Wall* (2020) by Remy Lai, Pan Macmillan; *The Mostly True Adventures of Matthew and Trim* (2005) by Cassandra Golds and Stephen Axelsen, Penguin; *The Secret Army: Operation Loki* (2006) by Sophie Masson and Anthony Davis, ABC Books; *The Great Gatsby* (2007) and *Hamlet* (2010), graphic novel adaptations by Nicki Greenberg, Allen & Unwin.

GENERAL WRITING TIPS

- Plan your story concept carefully; don't just rely on a synopsis. While it's good to suggest one or two aspects of physical appearance, leave the actual visual interpretation open. And remember, dialogue is the most important part of characterisation as far as the words are concerned.
- Think carefully about page extent and how your story will work out over the number of pages you are thinking of. The large format picture book style can be between 32 to 48 pages and even longer in the smaller novel-sized formats.
- Discuss the visual concept early on with the illustrator and publisher; don't be prescriptive of course, as this is very much a collaboration, but do indicate the general atmosphere you are hoping to convey. Work closely with them if you can and be ready to compromise but also be ready to stand firm where necessary.
- Vary points of view to make it seem less like 'and then this happened ... and then this ...' But obviously, too many points of view leads to chaos.

Advice from writers

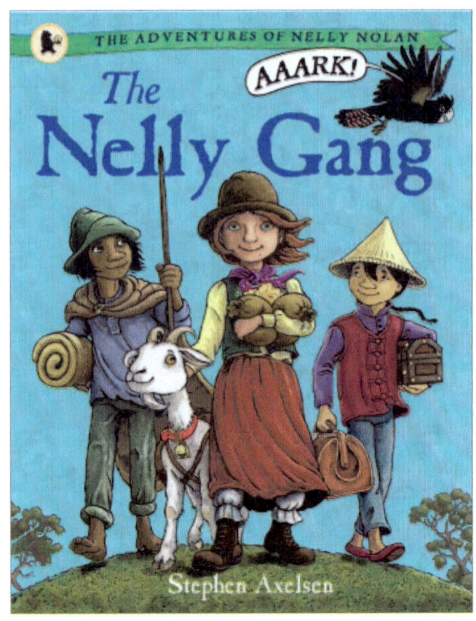

The process:

I'm from a French background, and I was brought up reading BDs, as we called them (short for bandes dessinées). So it's not surprising that as a kid the first 'books' I wrote (and illustrated) were BDs about the adventures of a character called Alicia who had two things I wanted: magic powers and long blonde hair. It was quite a long time into my adult writing career that a wonderful publisher took on the story that was to become my graphic novel with illustrator Anthony Davis, *The Secret Army: Operation Loki*. My first draft was written like a play script, complete with stage directions and dialogue; I had originally intended the directions to be scrapped, with only a few lines of narrative remaining, à la *Tintin*. But as I worked with the illustrator and publisher, it became clear this would be a different style of graphic novel to the BDs I'd grown up with, and it was intriguing to me as a writer to see how that developed. **— Sophie Masson, author**

Why I love graphic novels:

The reading, or viewing, of a good graphic novel is a filmic experience, one in which the story and the art can be enjoyed at one's own pace. There is space for a lot of content and for delighting in the sweep of the illustrations and narrative. And in the making of *The Nelly Gang*, I was able to immerse myself in the colours, costumes and scruffy fecundity of a nineteenth century Australian goldfield. **— Stephen Axelsen, authorstrator**

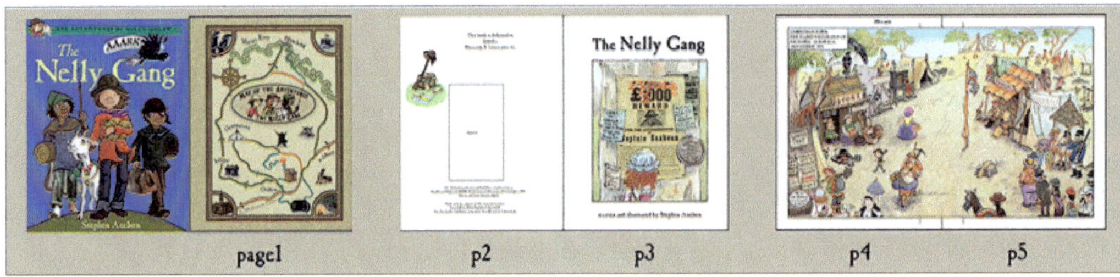

CHAPTER BOOKS AND JUNIOR FICTION

CHAPTER BOOKS AND JUNIOR FICTION GENERALLY COVER A READERSHIP AGE OF BETWEEN 5 TO 9 YEARS OLD.

While many readers of that age still read picture books, they are beginning to like longer ones too, although some aren't quite ready to leap the lengths of middle-grade. Of course, because reading abilities vary so much from child to child, texts may differ in length and complexity, so these books will generally be from 5,000 to 20,000 words and are written in many different genres.

Unsurprisingly, chapter books (sometimes known as 'early readers') are the first books that children read that have chapters in them. They are 'mini-novels' with a small number of short, sharp chapters (from 7 to 12 chapters are common) and generally only 5,000 to 7,000 words long with at least one or two illustrations (usually black and white) per chapter. These illustrations can be laid out in several ways: full page, half page, inset or even with the text wrapped around them.

Fantasy and humour are very common genres for these books, as are family and school stories. They may be published in a different size to other junior fiction and middle-grade books – often in larger dimensions and a slightly bigger print. And they are always attractive books, with bright covers and snappy titles.

Junior fiction books are the next step in the reading ladder. They are slightly longer than chapter books and start to use elements that are more sophisticated in areas such as content and language, but still in an age-appropriate way. A mix of narratives – such as diary entries, letters and emails – may also occur.

Junior fiction books have illustrations but perhaps not as many as in chapter books; however, that varies greatly, and graphic novels may be found in this age group (see 'Graphic novels' on page 10). Junior fiction books still need to have appealing covers and a larger font than in books for older readers. They are usually between 10,000 and 20,000 words long but may sometimes be from 25,000 to 30,000 words.

Illustrated fiction for younger readers (whether chapter books or junior fiction) has a long history in Australia and some classics are listed on the next page. Series are common, often featuring in contemporary Australian bestseller lists, for example, the *Treehouse* series (2011–2018) by Andy Griffiths, illustrated by Terry Denton, Pan Macmillan; *Ninja Kid* series (2018 onwards) by Anh Do, illustrated by Jeremy Ley and Anton Emdin, Scholastic; *Billie B Brown* (2010 onwards) and *Hey Jack!* (2012 onwards) series by Sally Rippin, illustrated by Aki Fukuoka, Hardie Grant; *Alice-Miranda* series (2010 onwards) and *Clementine Rose* series (2012–2019) by Jacqueline Harvey, illustrated by Anne Yi, Penguin.

Occasionally, you may also find single-author collections or multi-author anthologies of short stories in junior fiction. You will find more on these in 'Illustrated storybooks' (page 6) and 'Fiction anthologies' (page 8).

CHECK OUT

Some of the classic chapter books and junior fiction titles still in print: *The Magic Pudding* (first published 1918) written and illustrated by Norman Lindsay; *The Complete Adventures of Snugglepot and Cuddlepie* (first published 1918) written and illustrated by May Gibbs; *The Muddle-Headed Wombat* series (first published 1962) by Ruth Park and Noela Young; *Penny Pollard* series (first published 1983) by Robin Klein and Ann James; *Tashi* series (first published 1995) by Anna Fienberg and Kim Gamble.

A small selection of recent chapter book series (aside from the ones mentioned in the introduction):

TooCool and *Marcy* series (2013 onwards) respectively written by Phil Kettle and Susan Halliday, both illustrated by Tom Jellett, Ford Street Publishing; *Danny Best* series (2015 onwards) by Jen Storer, illustrated by Mitch Vane, HarperCollins; *Fizz* series (2016) by Lesley Gibbes and Stephen Michael King, Hardie Grant; *Lemonade Jones* series (2018–2019) by Davina Bell, illustrated by Karen Blair, Allen & Unwin.

An additional selection of recent junior fiction series:

Edie's Experiments (2020) by Charlotte Barkla, illustrated by Sandy Flett, Penguin; *Ella Diaries and Olivia's Secret Scribbles* series (2015 onwards) by Meredith Costain, illustrated by Danielle McDonald, Scholastic; *Deadly D and Justice Jones* (2013–2015) by Scott Prince and David Hartley, Magabala Books; *The Sorcerer's Tower* omnibus (2017) by Ian Irvine, illustrated by D. M. Cornish, Second Look Publishing; *Aussie Kids* series (2020) various authors and illustrators, Penguin Books.

A small selection of recent stand-alone chapter books and junior fiction novels:

The Adventures of Catvinkle (2020) by Elliot Perlman, illustrated by Laura Stitzel, Penguin; *Princess Hayley's Comet* (2018) by Rebecca Fung, illustrated by Kathy Creamer, Christmas Press; *The Tales of Mrs Mancini* (2016) and *The Fairy Dancers* (2015) by Natalie Jane Prior and Cheryl Orsini, both HarperCollins; *The Adventures of Jelly Bean* (2018) by Bill Condon and Dianne Bates, UQP; *Fil and Harry* (2021) by Jenny Blackford, illustrated by Kristin Devine, Christmas Press.

Advice from an agent

First and foremost, I want to be transported to another place/time/world when reading children's junior and middle-grade fiction. It's important for me to read things as a reader first to see if they speak to me – then I think about it from an agent's point of view. Unique and engaging voices, new experiences, the potential for escapism and stories that reflect all children's lives in some ways are things I look for. **— Pippa Masson, head of agents, Curtis Brown**

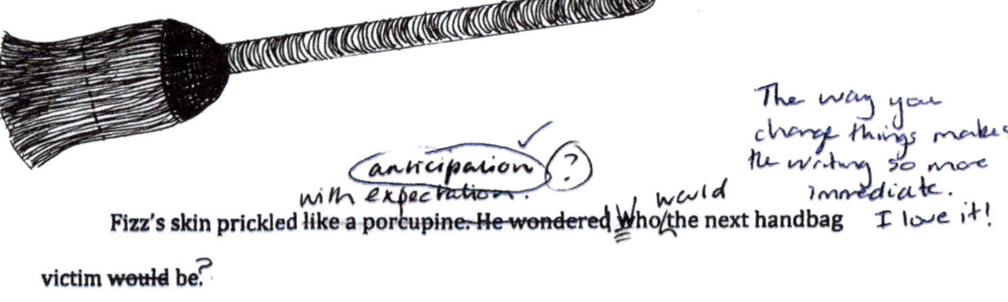

Fizz's skin prickled like a porcupine. He wondered who the next handbag victim would be.

'I'm sorry, Fizz,' said Sergeant Stern, holding up a photograph of a white Bolognese. 'The Handbag Kidnapper's latest victim is Crystal.'

Fizz gasped. Crystal was his sister. She was the handbag dog for a famous actress and always at red carpet events. Fizz's family had been worried about her safety ever since the first kidnapping.

'I'm so sorry, Fizz,' whispered Remi giving Fizz a comforting nuzzle.

'Me too,' said Amadeus.

Fizz blinked back his tears.

'What happened?' he asked.

Advice from writers

Phoebe McArthur is the pen-name of two writers, creating collaboratively. Their first published work was the popular chapter book *Lucy Newton, Little Witch* (2018, Christmas Press), which was shortlisted in the 2019 Speech Pathology Australia Book of the Year Awards. Here they write about how they went about creating the story:

Once upon a time, there was a mother–daughter writing team. One would start the story and the other would interrupt (sometimes quite rudely) to add her own ideas. To make things easier and stop talking over one another, they started to write their stories down, using track changes instead of cutting off each other's sentences. They'd bounce these documents back and forth, making changes until they were happy with the result. However, when it came to publishing time, they realised that neither of them knew who had written what. After having a good laugh, they decided to send it off to the publisher under one name: Phoebe McArthur, who seems to be the person that both of them want to be when they grow up.

The importance of character in junior fiction series:

My top tip for writing a compelling series for young readers is to make sure you start with a strong character who will present you with enough ideas to come up with plot lines for an undefined number of books. Initially, when I wrote the *Billie B Brown* series, I had no idea that I would end up writing 25 stories about one character, but, fortunately, she is complex and interesting enough to have kept me engaged over the years. Billie is pro-active, extroverted and a risk-taker, which made coming up with plot lines for her fairly easy. However, when it came to giving her best friend Jack his own series, this was more challenging as he had only ever been created to be Billie's sidekick and is less likely to take the initiative in any given situation. I had to work much harder to explore other strengths that could be found in a character who is quiet, introverted and risk-averse. — **Sally Rippin**

GENERAL WRITING TIPS

- Chapter books and junior fiction are short (even very short!) novels and need to work like that – they are not elongated picture book texts. Each chapter needs to build on the one before.
- Characters are of paramount importance and should be immediately appealing and distinctive.
- The plot needs to be simple, but strong and surprising! Best not to have sub-plots, but twists and turns are good.
- The world of your story should be quickly established; illustrations will help to convey a lot, so you don't need to describe too much. Ditto for characters – illustrations will help readers to visualise them, so you don't need to describe their physical appearance in detail.
- Pace should be brisk and language both accessible and lively. A light touch is essential! You can have great wordplay in a chapter book but keep it simple. Don't use complicated sentence structures.
- The beginning needs to propel you right into the action and the ending needs to be satisfying and complete, even if you are planning a sequel.

The inspiration for my first children's book, the chapter book *Princess Hayley's Comet*:

I was inspired to write *Princess Hayley's Comet* when looking up at the night sky and wondering 'what if?' When I was younger, I read a lot of science and science fiction books, and they made me curious about the world and beyond, and excited about the potential for wild adventures. The universe always held more wonders the further I explored. I hope my writing ignites others' curiosity and imagination, just as amazing stories and interesting facts fascinated and tantalised me. **— Rebecca Fung**

The importance of names:

One often-overlooked trick in character development – particularly when you have limited space – is to get the name right. Names have meanings, and they imply things about age, social background and ethnic origins. When we meet someone for the first time, their name is usually one of the first things we learn about them, and, whether we realise it or not, we use it to make assumptions (just think of all those unfortunate women called Karen). When you choose a name for your character, think carefully about what it will tell the reader and use that to your advantage. **— Natalie Jane Prior**

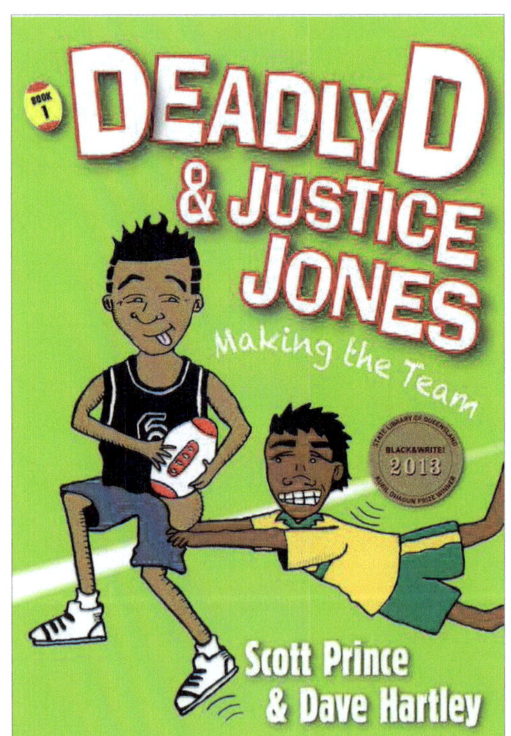

The importance of pace and humour:

Junior fiction series are often illustrated, so there's no need to spend too much time on description. Keep things moving at a fast pace with lots of short chapters and hooks to keep the pages turning. A dash of humour always works well and keeps things light and upbeat. **— Meredith Costain**

Language in chapter books:

Decoding words and sentences to gain meaning is tiring for a beginner reader. Be sure to support them with appropriate language, loads of illustration and a story that's worth the effort. **— Lesley Gibbes**

Writing great fantasy for junior (and middle-grade) readers:

It's all about knowing: knowing what your protagonist wants desperately, knowing who (or what) is doing everything possible to stop your protagonist from achieving their goal and knowing how high the cost will be if your protagonist fails. **— Ian Irvine**

MIDDLE-GRADE FICTION

FIRST, LET'S DEFINE WHAT 'MIDDLE-GRADE FICTION' MEANS. AT ITS MOST BASIC, IT MEANS BOOKS FOR READERS AGED FROM AROUND 9 TO 13 YEARS.

Children read these books after they graduate from chapter books and junior fiction, and before they start to tackle young adult (YA) fiction. Of course, what works for a 9 year old might not work so well for a 12 or 13 year old, and vice versa, so within that broad category of middle-grade, there are subcategories of lower and upper-middle-grade fiction (sometimes the lower end blurs with junior fiction and the upper end is referred to as 'tweens').

However, the age of the readership is only a rough guide. It's not about length, either: middle-grade fiction varies from around 30,000 to 70,000 words, with fantasy sometimes extended further than that. And finally, it's not about genre.

Middle-grade fiction covers all genres, from realism to fantasy, humour to historical, mystery to sports, and many more besides.

Series are popular in middle-grade fiction, but many stand-alone novels do very well, too. Some middle-grade books are illustrated and others are not. So, rather than one thing, middle-grade is an alchemy of many elements that indicates a story is for the target age range instead of their older siblings – or, indeed, their younger ones.

What is certain is that middle-grade is the golden age of reading, for this is where you find the most readers of all, and readers who are happy to range widely over genres and authors.

It's a great area for writers to work in because publishers are always on the lookout for good middle-grade fiction. And, especially in the fantasy and mystery genres, middle-grade fiction travels well. Note, for example, the international success of series such as Jessica Townsend's *Nevermoor*, John Flanagan's *Ranger's Apprentice*, R. A. Spratt's *Friday Barnes*, Lian Tanner's *The Keepers*, Emily Rodda's *Deltora Quest*, and Garth Nix and Sean Williams' *Have Sword, Will Travel.*

Single-author illustrated short story collections may also be found in the middle-grade area and are often very popular. For a small selection, see our list.

CHECK OUT

Four classic Australian middle-grade novels:

Hating Alison Ashley (first published 1984) by Robin Klein; *To the Wild Sky* (first published 1967) by Ivan Southall; *Playing Beatie Bow* (first published 1980) by Ruth Park; *The Nargun and the Stars* (first published 1973) by Patricia Wrightson.

Australian writers have always excelled in middle-grade fiction. Ranging from realistic school drama to hair-raising adventure, from time-slips into old Sydney to extraordinary fantasy, these four great Australian middle-grade novels are part of a long and rich tradition. They all received major awards in their time and are all still in print.

A small selection of some recent Australian middle-grade fiction:

Illustrated middle-grade fiction: *Stella Montgomery* series (2014–2019) written and illustrated by Judith Rossell, HarperCollins; *Pierre's Not There* (2020) written by Ursula Dubosarsky and illustrated by Christopher Nielsen, Allen & Unwin; *The Beast of Hushing Wood* (2017) written and illustrated by Gabrielle Wang, Penguin.

Realistic middle-grade fiction: *Black Cockatoo* (2018) by Carl Merrison and *Hakea Hustler*, Magabala; *Red* (2012) by Libby Gleeson, Allen & Unwin; *Hotaka* (2017) by John Heffernan, Allen & Unwin; *The Snow Pony* (2021) by Alison Lester, Allen & Unwin.

Middle-grade historical fiction: *Heroes of the Secret Underground* (2021) by Susanne Gervay, HarperCollins; *Cuckoo's Flight* (2021) by Wendy Orr, Allen & Unwin; *Tomodachi: The Forest of the Night* (2019) by Simon Higgins, Eagle Books; *Pirate Boy of Sydney Town* (2019) by Jackie French, HarperCollins.

Humorous middle-grade fiction: *Don't Follow Vee* (2019) by Oliver Phommavanh, Penguin; *Pie in the Sky* (2019) by Remy Lai, Walker Books; *The Romance Diaries: Ruby* (2013) by Jenna Austen, HarperCollins; *Secrets of a Schoolyard Millionaire* (2019) by Nat Amoore, Penguin.

Middle-grade fantasy: *Impossible Quest* series (2018–2020) by Kate Forsyth, Scholastic Australia; *Ghost Town* series (2017–2019) by Michael Pryor, Allen & Unwin; *The Grandest Bookshop in the World* (2020) by Amelia Mellor, Affirm Press; *Tarin of the Mammoths* (2017–2018) by Jo Sandhu, Penguin.

Middle-grade mystery fiction: *Riddle Gully Secrets* (2014) by Jen Banyard, Fremantle Press; *The Detective's Guide to Ocean Travel* (2021) by Nicki Greenberg, Affirm Press; *Charlie Chaplin: The Usual Suspect* (2021) by Phoebe McArthur, Christmas Press; *Kensy and Max* series (2018 onwards) by Jacqueline Harvey, Penguin.

Middle-grade single-author short story collections: *Spookiest Stories* (2007) by Paul Jennings, Penguin; *Give Peas a Chance and other Funny Stories* (2007) by Morris Gleitzman, Penguin; *Mr Bambuckle's Remarkables* (2017) by Tim Harris, Random House Australia.

GENERAL WRITING TIPS

- Think about the age of your characters. Main characters aged around 11 or 12 years are common in middle-grade fiction, and readers like to read slightly 'up,' so you might also find important characters in their teen years. Younger characters are also included but usually function as an annoyance or a source of humour. Adult characters are used too but are usually parents, teachers, mentors – or enemies!
- Construct a good plot – middle-grade readers will turn away from a book if it doesn't go at a good pace. That doesn't mean they don't respond to well-crafted writing and well-drawn characters because they certainly do. But don't concentrate so much on prose style that you forget about pace and plot!
- Use inventive, sparkling language and concepts – readers of this age appreciate a bright, fresh voice, clever ideas and wordplay.
- Add humour – even in a more 'serious' novel, a playful touch of humour goes a long way with this age group!
- And of course – read, read, READ! Have a look at some of the examples of great middle-grade fiction we've listed, but don't limit yourself to that. There's a wealth of wonderful reads to discover.

Check out the wonderful podcast series *Middle Grade Mavens* for many more reading ideas!

Advice from writers

Inspiration: Jenny Blackford's middle-grade novel, *The Girl in the Mirror* (2019, Eagle Books) won the 2020 Davitt Award for Best Children's Crime Novel. Here she talks about being inspired by an old mirror she was once given and the 1890s house she once lived in:

That mirror was at least a hundred years old. How many faces had it seen, over the years? And my workroom, in that old house, was a bedroom at the back of the upper storey. If, sometimes, while I worked into the evening in that back bedroom, I heard strange creakings on the stairs, how could I not wonder about the family who lived there, back when the house was new?

Bertie's ghost raced down the stairs again, laughing. Clarissa heard, but she just kept on working at her horrid embroidery: "All Things Bright and Beautiful". The harder she tried to get it right, the more the sheep that she was sewing under the words looked like a large woolly rat. Aunt Lily would sneer at her work again. Sigh.

Clarissa's older brother Alfred learnt Latin and Natural Science at a private school for boys, but Aunt Lily said that it was a wicked waste, educating girls. She'd always said, "Your duty, girl, is to marry and produce sons for the British Empire, just like our dear Queen Victoria."

BA **Beattie Alvarez**
Italics for thoughts are removed because of our house style.

Writing action scenes:

Convincing action scenes call for three things: ignoring TV and movie fight scene tropes, knowing what your characters could – and would – do and scientific blow-by-blow planning. **— Simon Higgins**

Tomodachi The Forest of the Night edited SM - Saved to this PC

Unfortunately, his courage to speak evaporated along with it. Another time, he told himself, and soon. Another time when Kenji was away.

Daniel snorted to himself. ~~gave a subtle sneer.~~ Who cared what Kenji might make of this anyhow? At times, depending on his mood, the young warrior was visibly jealous of Daniel and Otsu's friendship. ~~Daniel gave a determined nod.~~ Well, *that* would have to come to an end really soon or –

He jumped as Otsu flinched and quickly sat bolt upright. Wild eyes darted in

First things:

The aim of the first draft is to finish the first draft. All other more lofty aims – your vision for the story, the subtext you want to weave in, the views you want to share – are secondary. You'll never achieve these or even get published if you don't finish the first draft, so knuckle down, grit your teeth and get the job done! — **Michael Pryor**

Creating great characters:

Character drives all my longer fiction. Focus on your character's feelings, wants and needs. Not all may enter the book, but you need to know them. And then rewrite till there is not one unnecessary word in your story. — **Libby Gleeson**

Research:

Research is a fabulous part of writing historical fiction but never forget that you are not writing a history book. Once you have done your research, put it away. Then write your novel with fabulous characters on their story journey. That doesn't mean you shouldn't go back to check historical information or discover new information during your writing. However, story first. — **Susanne Gervay**

Titles:

I love the title of *The Detective's Guide to Ocean Travel* because it has all the right ingredients of sleuthing, excitement and the flavour of the golden age of ocean voyages, and it references a 'Lady's Guide' that features in the story. The title fits the book like a glove. Amazingly, we only arrived at this name when the book was almost ready to go to print. For most of its life, my manuscript was titled Aquitania after the ship on which it is set. But my very cluey publishers wanted a more dynamic title to capture the tone of the story. — **Nicki Greenberg**

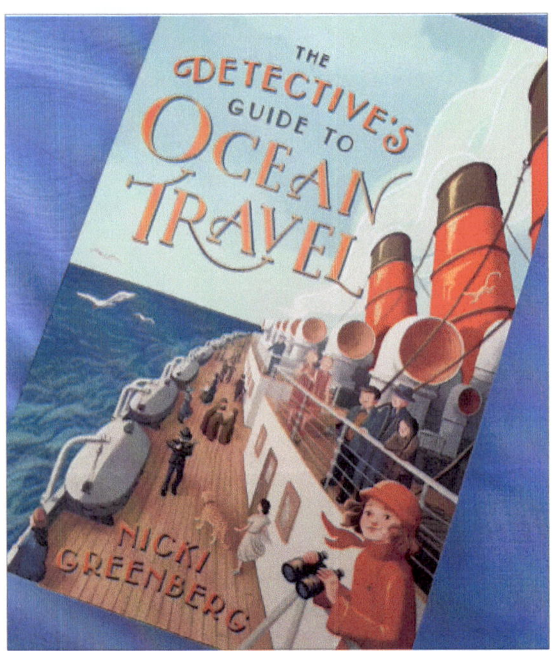

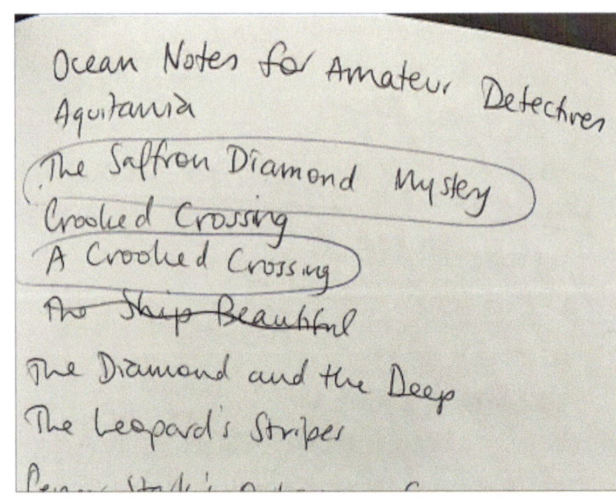

John Heffernan on why he loves writing middle-grade fiction:

Your audience is ready to be receptive, with an inherent appetite to discover, explore, absorb and wonder about life. Our task as authors is to not only feed that appetite but to make it grow.

Award-winning translator Stephanie Smee has translated several children's middle-grade classics, from French and Swedish to English. Here she writes about the challenges:

Translating children's classics is a privilege and a delight, but they are beloved classics for a reason, and the translator's task is to understand why they have become classics. Translators are always looking for the 'voice' – be it of the author or their characters. It is probably the most significant challenge. The voices, the humour, the inflections, the rhythms, are the things we are trying to emulate, to bring from one language to another. Our task is to render the text in such a way that it feels as fresh to our new readers as it has done to the children who have been enjoying the beloved originals for so many years.

Advice from publishers

What publishers look for:

Even in my free time, I predominantly read children's books, so I'm well versed in what makes good children's fiction, whether for middle-grade or younger readers. Basically, I'm looking for books that I want to read. Ones with great characters, good stories and not too many obvious lessons intended to teach the reader. I'm never opposed to a mystery or adventure, but they aren't requirements as long as the books are well written. **— Beattie Alvarez, commissioning editor, Christmas Press**

Nothing excites me more than a pitch from a creator that taps into a personal, lived experience and delivers a story that makes it enjoyable and relatable to a broader audience. When a creator starts with this sort of authenticity, it always shines through their work. Additionally, it guarantees that when they talk about their work with readers, booksellers and media, it greatly helps audiences connect with the story. **— Tash Besliev, publisher, Children's Books, Affirm Press**

Eva Mills, publishing director, Books for Children and Young Adults, Allen & Unwin, shares her tips for what to avoid in writing middle-grade fantasy:

Middle-grade fantasy is one of my favourite genres to publish, but I'm very picky about it. Here are my top bugbears:

- Surreal fantasy worlds in which anything can happen. The world might be magical, but the magic still needs a strong underlying logic and consistency, otherwise your reader will be left rudderless and there is no sense of suspense.
- Weak or overblown world building. There's a fine line between knowing your world well enough to convey a sense to the reader that it is real and overloading them with too much information. You don't need to put every tiny detail on the page, but if you don't know your world, then how can you expect the reader to believe in it?
- Stereotypical characters. Literally, anything goes in a fantasy world, so why perpetuate damaging tropes about powerful men, passive women and suppressed minorities? The best fantasy is a little bit political as well as entertaining, challenging us to think about the real world in a different way.

NON-FICTION

NON-FICTION IS A RICH AND DIVERSE AREA OF CHILDREN'S BOOK PUBLISHING IN AUSTRALIA, EVEN IF, HISTORICALLY, IT HAS NOT RECEIVED AS MUCH ATTENTION AS FICTION AND PICTURE BOOKS. UNTIL THE EVE POWNALL AWARD, ESTABLISHED IN 1988 IN HONOUR OF THE DISTINGUISHED WRITER EVE POWNALL, NON-FICTION FOR CHILDREN DID NOT HAVE A SPECIFIC CATEGORY IN THE CHILDREN'S BOOK COUNCIL OF AUSTRALIA'S INFLUENTIAL ANNUAL AWARDS LIST.

That doesn't mean it was completely ignored. Eve Pownall's classic non-fiction book for children, *The Australia Book*, illustrated by Margaret Senior and first published in 1952 (reprinted 2008), won the Older Readers category in the Children's Book Council Awards in that year. Popular and influential, it was a departure in non-fiction publishing for children at the time, focusing on profuse illustrations and reading pleasure as much as information.

Educational publishers took the lead early on in creating non-fiction books for children, with a sprinkling of excellent titles from trade publishers from the 1980s onwards. A few of these are still in print, such as Nadia Wheatley and Donna Rawlinson's *My Place* (1987), but today there has been a big growth in non-fiction, with many publishers releasing great new books on all kinds of subjects.

Publishers of children's non-fiction range from big to medium to small publishers, with a few, such as Melbourne-based Wild Dog, specialising in children's non-fiction. Authors known principally for their fiction have also written acclaimed non-fiction books, for example, Ursula Dubosarsky and Tohby Riddle's award-winning *Word Spy* duology, which has also sold internationally, and Jackie French's series of picture books with Bruce Whatley around extreme natural disasters such as droughts, floods, fires and cyclones.

Some non-fiction authors, however, specialise in the genre, such as writer-illustrator Sami Bayly, with her unique illustrated encyclopedias, and writer-photographer Jan Latta, with her popular *True to Life* series

GENERAL WRITING TIPS

- If you want to write in this field, follow the expert tips offered by successful writers of non-fiction from these pages and read, read, read! We've listed some great examples of children's non-fiction in check out, but you don't need to limit yourself to these.
- A good place to start exploring is to have a look at the Eve Pownall shortlists and notable books over the last few years. You can find these on the Children's Book Council of Australia website: www.cbca.org.au.

about wild animals. Non-fiction for children isn't one size fits all, either. It covers ages from babyhood right through to upper-middle grade and can come in board books, picture books, narratives, encyclopedias, compendiums and other forms. It can feature illustrations, photographs or a mix of the two.

It can cover science, arts, history, autobiography and biography, culture, sport, the natural world and pretty much anything else you can think of. There is certainly nothing dry or boring about contemporary non-fiction writing for children, with playfulness, humour and gripping narratives as important as in fiction, along with meticulous research, of course. It is a very interesting field for writers to consider, and publishers are on the lookout for good non-fiction for children.

CHECK OUT

Four classic non-fiction books for children:

The Australia Book (first published 1952, republished 2008) written by Eve Pownall and illustrated by Margaret Senior; *My Place* (first published 1987, still in print) by Nadia Wheatley and Donna Rawlins; *Tucker* (first published 1994, still in print) written and illustrated by Ian Abdulla; *My Girragundji* (first published 1998, still in print) by Boori Monty Pryor and Meme McDonald.

A small selection of contemporary non-fiction for children:

Board books and picture books

The ABC Book of Cars, Trains, Boats and Planes (2010) written by Helen Martin and Judith Simpson, illustrated by Cheryl Orsini, HarperCollins; *Do Not Lick This Book* (2017) written by Idan Ben-Barak and illustrated by Julian Frost, Allen & Unwin; *Dry to Dry: The Seasons of Kakadu* (2020) written by Pamela Freeman and illustrated by Liz Anelli, Walker Books Australia; *Mopoke* (2017) written and illustrated by Philip Bunting, Omnibus; *Cyclone* (2016) written by Jackie French and illustrated by Bruce Whatley, Scholastic; *Matthew Flinders: Adventures on Leaky Ships* (2021) written by Carole Wilkinson and illustrated by Prue Pittock, Wild Dog.

Photographic picture books

Our Birds: Ŋilimurruŋgu Wäyin Malanynha (2018) by Siena Stubbs, Magabala Books; *True to Life* series (1995 to now) by Jan Latta, True to Life Books; *Australian Story: An Illustrated Timeline* (2017) by Tania McCartney, National Library of Australia.

Compendium and encyclopedia-style non-fiction

The Word Spy (2008) and *Return of the Word Spy* (2010) by Ursula Dubosarsky and Tohby Riddle, Penguin; *The Illustrated Encyclopaedia of Ugly Animals* (2019) and *The Illustrated Encyclopaedia of Dangerous Animals* (2020) written and illustrated by Sami Bayly, Lothian/Hachette Australia; *Australia Survival Guide* (2019) and *Human Body Survival Guide* (2020) by George Ivanoff, Penguin; *Australian Kids through the Years* (2016) by Tania McCartney and Andrew Joyner, National Library of Australia.

Junior and middle-grade narrative non-fiction

Boomerang and Bat: The Story of the Real First Eleven (2016) by Mark Greenwood and Terry Denton, Allen & Unwin; the *Aussie STEM Star* series (2020–2021) various authors, Wild Dingo Press; *The Gallipoli Story* (2015) by Patrick Carlyon, Allen & Unwin; *Maralinga's Long Shadow* (2016) by Christobel Mattingley, Allen & Unwin; *Kicking Goals with Goodesy and Magic* (2016) by Anita Heiss, with Adam Goodes and Michael O'Loughlin, Black Inc./Piccolo Nero; *Lennie the Legend: Solo to Sydney by Pony* (2020) by Stephanie Owen Reeder, National Library of Australia.

Advice from writers and authorstrators

Creating non-fiction books:

Neither overestimate nor underestimate the knowledge of the child readership. Children love discovery, so they will be happy to find out! But they will lose interest if they feel condescended to or if there is no discovery involved. It's about building on their knowledge and adding to it, in a way that makes sense and enriches their understanding. With the *Word Spy* books, I tried all the time to follow the well-known aphorism, 'As simple as possible, but no simpler.' My goal was to keep it true but in a form that was not overwhelmingly and unnecessarily complex. Of course, be extremely conscientious about your research. Don't let things pass that you are not 100 per cent sure of. It's a headache, checking everything, but it's not negotiable. Remember, a non-fiction book should not just be a collection of interesting facts – we have Google for that. A good non-fiction book has a crafted narrative as much as any fiction book – it has its own shape and sense of direction. — **Ursula Dubosarsky**

The hard part about writing non-fiction is that there is so much misinformation out there. So, always check your sources! And look for interesting ways to present the information. So, for example, rather than a large slab of fact-heavy text, I'll weave the info into a narrative or use a fictional character or simply set out the information in bite-sized chunks. — **George Ivanoff**

Research heavily influences my illustration process. Finding out the details behind each and every creature ultimately changes the layout, elements in focus and most importantly, whether to include it at all. I find a crucial part of scientific illustration is the ability to use all of the available resources to help you construct a visual piece that allows the audience to easily digest the information. Deep diving into the science and background of an animal allows me to carefully decide which facts to include, resulting in an artwork that is modelled around my words and a spread that is both entertaining and informative. — **Sami Bayly**

Advice from publishers

Cathi Lewis at Wild Dingo Press on the concept and creation of the *Aussie STEM Star* series:

I envisaged a ripping tale – like a novel rather than non-fiction, so with a strong narrative style and arc, and approximately 10 to 15 chapters. To this end we commissioned children's writers of fiction and non-fiction to write on each STEM* star, and an illustrator to sprinkle 2 to 3 illustrations through each chapter to break up the text, pique interest, and illustrate things the reader may not be familiar with. The format, both in extent and book size, was based on similar publications for the age group – not too long (25,000 words) and not too intimidating for the more reluctant reader.

(*STEM is a common abbreviation for four connected areas of study: science, technology, engineering and mathematics.)

POETRY AND VERSE NOVELS

AUSTRALIAN WRITERS HAVE ALWAYS EXCELLED IN THE CREATION OF POETRY, FROM THE ROLLICKING BUSH BALLADS OF BANJO PATTERSON AND HENRY LAWSON TO THE STRIKING IMAGES OF LES MURRAY AND JUDITH WRIGHT.

But it's not only for adults that Australian writers have shown their affinity for poetry – from the fun nonsense rhymes of C. J. Dennis to the striking images of William Hart-Smith, from the sharp observations of Max Fatchen to the lyricism of Anne Bell – classic Australian poets have created works for children that have stood the test of time. Today, many excellent writers are working in this field, with their works published in *The School Magazine* (always a great supporter of children's poetry) in single-poet collections and multi-poet anthologies.

Verse novels are also another aspect of writing poetry, blending the strengths of both poetry and prose. Several contemporary Australian writers for children have created popular and award-winning works in this genre.

A good market for children's poets is *The School Magazine* – do consider submitting there. Many poems first published here have later been published in book form, in anthologies. Some have even been extended and transformed as picture book text, for example, Sophie Masson and Laura Wood's picture book *Building Site Zoo* (2017, Lothian Children's Books) started life as a poem published in *The School Magazine* https://theschoolmagazine.com.au/.

GENERAL WRITING TIPS

- Don't obsess about rhyme; rhythm is more important. Rhyme is great but the right rhythm will give that nice pattern and flow anyway.
- Have a single clear theme as the focus.
- Do be unexpected with image and idea, but don't strain after effect.
- Keep the poems relatively short.
- Be imaginatively observant of the natural world as a wonderful source of inspiration, but avoid cliché.
- Always keep your child self in mind!
- Explore specialist children's poetry sites, like: Australian Children's Poetry https://australianchildrenspoetry.com.au/, Australian Poetry Library https://www.poetrylibrary.edu.au/home (which has a section for children's poetry), The Children's Poetry Archive https://childrens.poetryarchive.org/, Poetry Foundation https://www.poetryfoundation.org/ and many others.

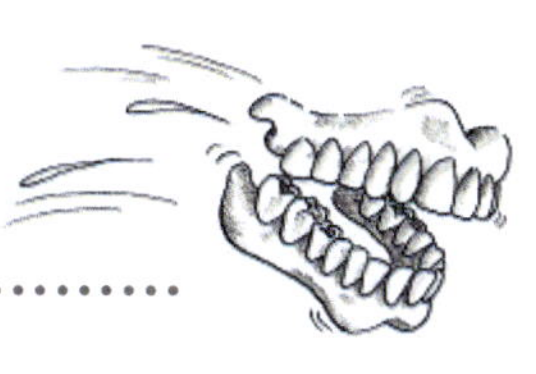

CHECK OUT

A small selection of classic Australian children's poetry collections and anthologies:

A Book for Kids (first published 1921) by C. J. Dennis; *A Pocketful of Rhymes* (first published 1989, republished 2017) by Max Fatchen; *Birds, Beasts, Flowers* (first published 1996) by William Hart-Smith; *Pardon my Garden: Verses for Young Children* (first published 1992) edited by Sally Odgers.

A small selection of recent anthologies and collections of poetry:

100 Ways to Fly (2019) by Michelle Taylor, UQP; *A Boat of Stars* (2018) edited by Margaret Connolly and Natalie Jane Prior, ABC Books; *Our Home is Dirt by Sea* (2016) selected by Dianne Bates, Walker Books; *This is Home: Essential Australian Poems for Children* (2019) selected by Jackie French and illustrated by Tania McCartney, National Library of Australia.

Eight little chicks having lots of fun.
Huit petits poussins s'amusent comme des fous.
Nine little chicks crowding all around to see —
Neuf petits poussins se bousculent pour mieux voir —
Ten little chicks, hungry, go off home,
Dix petits poussins rentrent chez eux bredouilles,
And one little wiggly worm escapes underground.
Et un petit ver tortillant s'échappe sous terre.

73

A small selection of verse novels (for middle-grade readers):

Pearl Verses the World (2009) by Sally Murphy, Walker Books; *Bleakboy and Hunter Stand Out in the Rain* (2014) and *Zoe, Max and the Bicycle Bus* (2020) both by Steven Herrick, UQP; *Footprints on the Moon* (2021) and *Leave Taking* (2018) both by Lorraine Marwood, UQP.

FOCUS ON VERSE NOVELS

Tips from Lorraine Marwood for aspiring verse novelists:

I love the deceptively simple yet profound layers one can achieve through poetry and subsequently verse novels. To me, it seems the best of both worlds – best of poetry strengths, best of prose strengths. Yet, the challenge is to make a balance between the two genres, so that there is a seamless blending and the result a great read with layers of emotional depth.

- Try writing shorter lines with a maximum of eight or nine words to a line, and vary the length of the lines.
- Use nouns and verbs as the building blocks of your writing – ensuring that no padding or flowery language invades like an unwanted weed. Every word counts in poetry and the verse novel.
- Invite the reader into your scene with sensory details. Can they smell that bonfire burning? Can they taste the barbeque? Can they feel the anger or the sense of loneliness your character feels?
- 'Show not tell' is vital in poetry and in the verse novel, where the narrative prose helps drive dialogue and action. Show us that grief; show us that longing or that unattainable wish.

Research also matters in fiction and a verse novel especially. In my historical verse novel, *Footprints on the Moon*, I made sure my facts around the Apollo 11 mission were correct, and the social attitudes and everyday lifestyle in 1969 Australia were as realistic as possible. This part of the verse novel is vital for that sense of authenticity for both the plot and character development.

We swing
and we sway
in a dare-devil way
on a hair-raising,
zig-zagging track.

Our father
once tried.
You'll find him
inside
with a very
large bruise
on his back.

Advice from poets

I love writing poetry because a poem enables me to capture a moment that has elicited an emotion be that joy, sadness or surprise. Poems allow me to share how a moment has made me feel. Poems are condensed, visual tastes of a poet's experience. **— Jackie Hosking**

Rhythm is a powerful storyteller. Use it to bring mood and meaning to your poems. **— Lesley Gibbes, poet in *A Boat of Stars***

Advice from editors and compilers

Poems should be about subjects that children can relate to, not adult topics. They should be easily understood and have an impact, giving the reader a wow moment. Avoid easy, predictable rhyme. Anyone can write ordinary, mediocre verse. The poems we remember are the ones in which the writer has laboured to find the absolute best words. Only by working hard will you stand out from the crowd. **— Dianne Bates, compiler of children's poetry anthology *Our Home is Dirt by Sea***

For *A Boat of Stars*, we looked for poems that modern Australian children would enjoy, and that reflected their experience of the world. We wanted poems that they would find engaging and amusing, and enjoy returning to, again and again. The book needed to be Australian in its outlook, so poems about Australian animals, and with Indigenous content, were essential. When we'd selected about two-thirds of the poems, we looked critically at what we had, and where there were gaps, and then asked a couple of experienced teachers to identify topics they thought would be useful in the classroom. **— Margaret Connolly and Natalie Jane Prior, editors of *A Boat of Stars*, ABC Books**

PLAYS

WRITING PLAYS FOR CHILDREN CAN BE A LOT OF FUN, BUT ALSO QUITE A BIT OF WORK, AND REQUIRES A GOOD UNDERSTANDING OF THEATRE. ALTHOUGH A PLAY MAY WELL FIND ITS WAY ONTO A STAGE, IT'S NOT OFTEN THAT A BOOK OF PLAYS SPECIFICALLY FOR CHILDREN IS PUBLISHED.

However, it is not altogether unheard of, as you'll learn in this chapter. *The School Magazine* is a great outlet for children's plays, and they will often publish several plays a year by different authors. A few are then turned into books, like Ursula Dubosarsky's plays based on Greek and Roman myths, *The Boy Who Could Fly and Other Magical Plays for Children* (2019, Christmas Press), which first appeared as individual plays in *The School Magazine*. Some plays may also be commissioned adaptations of famous children's fiction, such as Richard Tulloch's play based on Andy Griffiths and Terry Denton's *13-Storey Treehouse*.

If you want to write plays, you need to read them, of course! A good place to start is by checking out some of the books we recommend, as well as having a look at plays published in *The School Magazine*. You can also look up play scripts at Australian Plays Transform https://apt.org.au/ and search in the children's theatre category. And have a look at the great advice from children's playwrights on these pages as well!

CHECK OUT

Single-author collections:

This School is Driving Me Nuts and Other Funny Plays for Children, written by Duncan Ball and illustrated by Craig Smith (first published as *Funny Plays for Kids*, 1989) republished 2016, with an additional play and foreword by the author, Christmas Press. *The Boy Who Could Fly and Other Magical Plays for Children* (2019) written by Ursula Dubosarsky and illustrated by Amy Golbach, Christmas Press.

Plays based on other works:

The 13-Storey Treehouse: A play for young audiences (2019) adapted by Richard Tulloch from Andy Griffiths' and Terry Denton's bestselling book of the same name, NewSouth Plays; *Hating Alison Ashley: The play* (1988, still in print) adapted by Richard Tulloch from Robin Klein's classic children's novel of the same name, Penguin; *Blabbermouth: The play* (1994, still in print) adapted by Mary Morris from Morris Gleitzman's bestseller of the same name, Currency Press; *Hitler's Daughter, The play* (2007, still in print) adapted by Eva di Cesare, Sandra Eldridge and Tim McGarry, from Jackie French's popular novel of the same name, Currency Press.

(*Aside*) The moral of this story is that evil deeds will become a pain in the neck (*Slowly*) SUE NORA LAYTA. *Ffffffank* you very much.
(*FRANK bows*.)

CURTAIN

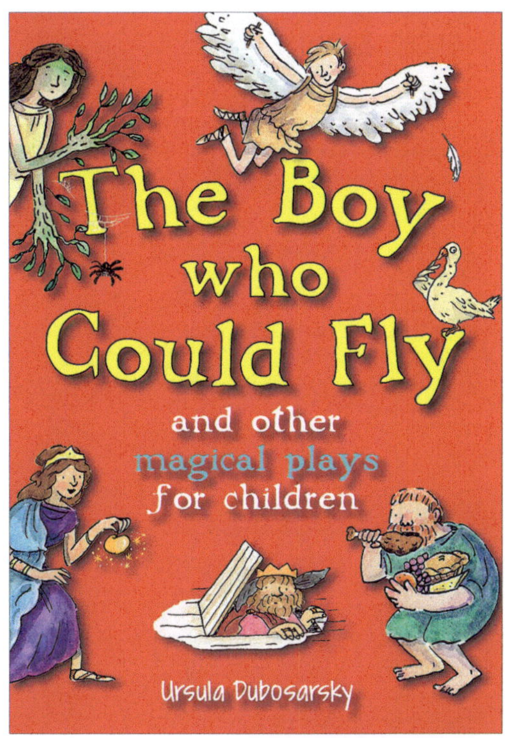

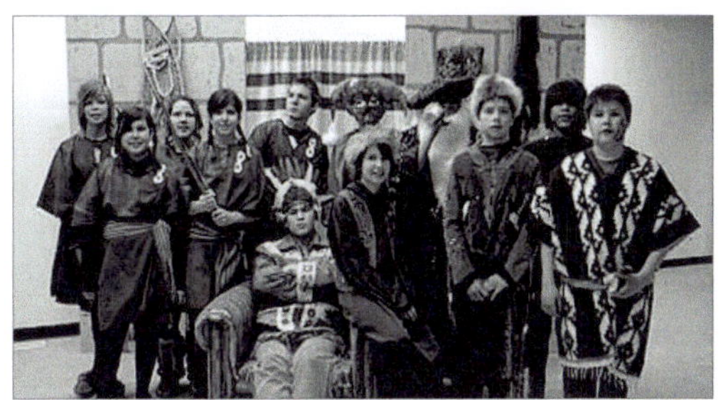

Advice from writers

Ursula Dubosarsky's three top tips for writing plays:

- If you're stuck for ideas, find a good strong plot line to work with and reinvent from fairy tales, myths and legends, and famous old stories. You can reinterpret them and make them your own.
- Remember, each character needs to speak with their own voice, not just one voice with different names attached! This is how you create your characters and make the play come alive. It will make it a richer reading experience, of course, but also much easier to act or to be read aloud by others.
- Simplify the action. Your play needs to be understood at a basic level by child (and adult) audiences as it is watched. The way we understand the spoken word is very different to the written word. It doesn't mean your play should be superficial – it just means that people need to know what is going on while it's happening. It can still leave them with a lot of complexity and thinking time after it's over. In fact, the greatest plays grip you completely while you are watching but leave you wondering afterwards.

Richard Tulloch's latest play is based on the phenomenal junior fiction bestseller by Andy Griffiths and Terry Denton, *The 13-Storey Treehouse*. Here he writes about the challenge and pleasure of writing a play based on famous books:

When a clever author has already taken care of the theme, setting, characters and plot, turning a popular book into a play should be a doddle. There's an excited audience waiting at the box office. They already know how the story ends. So the challenge is to make the theatre experience as rich and surprising as reading the book. But unless the story will benefit from what theatre can bring – visuals, sound, stage magic and the shared relationship between actors and audience – don't try an adaptation. Write an original play instead!

Duncan Ball shares his discoveries as former editor of *The School Magazine*:

It was while I was the editor of *The School Magazine* that I discovered that kids often liked reading the plays we published even more than reading the stories! The plays had plots and characters just like the stories but without long descriptive passages. Dialogue straight from the characters' mouths drove the stories along and let the reader feel what the characters were feeling. When I left *The School Magazine*, I decided to use my passion for terrible puns and other wordplays to write the collection of sketches and plays that was recently published as *This School is Driving Me Nuts and Other Funny Plays* for Kids, beautifully illustrated by Craig Smith.

ILLUSTRATING

PICTURE BOOKS

PICTURE BOOKS HAVE ALWAYS BEEN CONSIDERED BOOKS FOR YOUNG CHILDREN. IN RECENT YEARS, THIS IDEA HAS COMPLETELY CHANGED, AND NOW THERE IS AN ENORMOUS VARIETY OF SOPHISTICATED PICTURE BOOKS FOR ALL AGE GROUPS AND PLENTY OF EXAMPLES TO TEMPT, EXCITE AND CHALLENGE THE READER, WHETHER THEY ARE A CHILD OR AN ADULT.

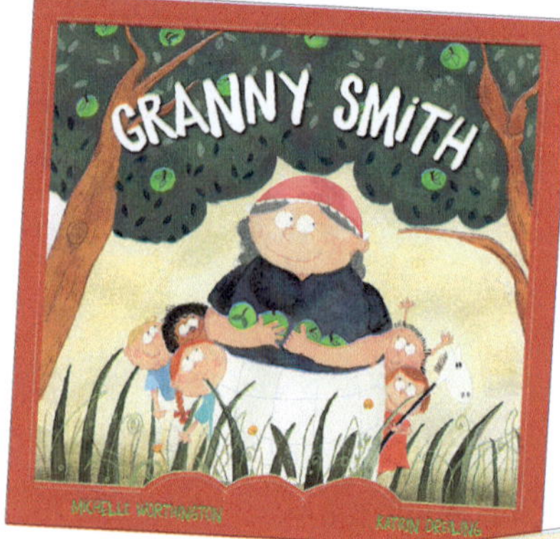

There's never been a better time to be making children's picture books. More books are being made than ever before, and publishers are investing in a wonderfully diverse spectrum of creators, styles and stories.
— Simon Howe

A pencil.

Picture books are usually the first introduction to art and culture for a young child, so parents will want to provide picture books by the best writers and illustrators. Agent Margaret Connolly's illustrator clients include Julie Vivas, Stephen Michael King, Matt Shanks, Cheryl Orsini, Sara Acton, Christopher Nielsen and many others. Here, Margaret describes what she looks for when taking on a new illustrator:

> I look for someone who can draw, whose work has something fresh and original and distinctive – someone whose style is very much their own, not imitative or generic. I look for that creative spark, for that joyful surprise that is part of the pleasure of discovering a new illustrator.
>
> And I look for someone easy to work with because I want to collaborate with them long term. Illustrators need patience and the will to keep going but also the capacity to listen and to be flexible. A sense of humour doesn't hurt, either! It's all part of what will help an illustrator build a sustainable career because it's never going to be easy.

Many artists have now become involved in creating picture books as a way of communicating and presenting their artwork, which has resulted in an abundantly diverse and exciting variety of imagery being presented to children and young people. Artwork in a picture book can provide children with an enjoyable, educational and memorable experience.

However, if the words don't interact with the pictures or the pictures are just duplicating the author's words, the book will not have succeeded in its shared narrative.

The same problem arises if the story is brilliantly entertaining, but the illustrations don't share, complement or add anything to the story, resulting in the pictures serving only as decorations. A successful picture book will be a balanced combination of lively text and unforgettable pictures to create a seamless narrative. When read aloud, it should delight children so much that repeat readings will be demanded.

The World's Worst Pirate (2017, Little Pink Dog Books), written by Michelle Worthington and illustrated by Katrin Dreiling, has lively, bouncy text with pictures that complement and expand the narrative. There is also a hilarious subplot in the background of the main visual narrative between the ship's cat and a parrot.

Katrin Dreiling explains her way of working:

> *The World's Worst Pirate* was the first picture book I had illustrated with a traditional publisher, namely Little Pink Dog Books, and with a team attached to the creative process. Before, I had self-published titles with little to no guidance. It is part of the reason *The World's Worst Pirate* will always be special to me, and I loved every minute of creating the illustrations.
>
> My illustration process has always been a wild mix of different techniques and media. I love to combine traditional with digital so that everything looks as handmade as possible. I often try to incorporate painting techniques that children are familiar with from kindy or school to inspire them to get 'hands-on creative' after looking at my picture books.
>
> Thanks to this tremendously positive first experience with a publisher, I have since been able to confidently explore and develop my style further because I felt my work was appreciated and respected. Such things can give you wings as an illustrator.
>
> Often it is a difficult balance, but I would encourage aspiring illustrators to keep an open mind when working in a publishing team. Consider ideas and suggestions from the 'other side' because that is where magic can happen. This requires trust and takes time to build. The best way to increase your confidence is to continuously work on your skills and take opportunities for personal development as much as possible. A good side effect is also that you're constantly busy, and there is no time to doubt yourself or wonder about your next (or first?) paid job.

Integrating pictures and words in children's books often results in generating multiple layers of meaning and different ways of reading messages. Unlike the words in picture books, the pictures are not read linearly.

They communicate using multi-layered visual 'codes' or 'signals', which include colour, contrast, tone, shape, form, texture, imagery and space.

When looking at the images in Georgie Donaghey's award-winning picture book *In the Shadow of an Elephant* (2019, Little Pink Dog Books), the illustrator, Sandra Severgnini, has made clever use of most of the aforementioned methods. White space helps to display the setting, movement, action, drama, texture and character.

The imagery should always present to the reader what the words don't say, and vice versa. Sandra explains her way of working:

I usually have a very clear vision of how the illustrations will look, so I don't do lots of small sketches. I prefer to work through it as I am doing the actual illustration. Any minor changes can be done with the help of the computer and tracing paper. I use a mix of either watercolour, Photoshop, colour pencils or (as in the case of *In the Shadow of an Elephant*) graphite pencil. I set up a page layout in Illustrator and lay all the JPG images out in this. In most cases, I will set up the type to see how it works with the illustrations. It gives a great overall view and is easy to send to the author and publisher for their feedback.

There is no secret formula to getting published. It's determination, patience, love for your work and, of course, a handful of luck! Every artist has a unique style, and it's this quality that a publisher is looking for. The artistic style will bring out the best in the chosen story. This is where luck comes in: it's having your work in the right place at the right time. So, send your folio out constantly, keep a current profile and good luck!

Feel your work from your heart! — **Sandra Severgnini**

Katrina Fisher describes her process of creating the visual narrative for Sophie Masson's picture book *A House of Mud* (2020, Little Pink Dog Books):

> I begin a new project by researching the topic of the story. For instance, with *A House of Mud*, I was provided with photographs taken by Sophie Masson when building her real mudbrick house with her family. I also researched mudbrick homes at the library and on the internet. I wanted to ensure the pictures and the processes were accurate. I spent some time developing the characters and deciding on the colours I would use. For this particular book, I used watercolour paint on paper.
>
> Once the paint was dry, I added details with coloured pencil. Last year, I purchased a Wacom drawing tablet, and this has been so beneficial. I can now create my storyboard and roughs on the computer (which works well for me) and then transfer the images to the watercolour paper, which I paint traditionally.

Clever interplay with words and images always makes for a satisfying picture book experience that will help the growth of a young child's imagination and aid their cognitive, emotional, aesthetic and intellectual development. It is only recently that pictorial literature has been given any credit for the importance of children's educational and emotional development. It has meant that even extremely difficult topics, such as depression, war, death or family violence, are being depicted.

These issues are presented calmly and sensitively in the safe and secure environment of a picture book story for a child to share with a trusted adult or teacher. Nicky Johnston illustrates the topic of domestic violence in a gentle and reassuring picture book story written by Dimity Powell, *At the End of Holyrood Lane* (2017, EK Books).

Nicky's delightfully whimsical and sensitive illustrations share the narrative by presenting violence as a gathering of dark clouds that block out the sunshine in the home life of a young child. The dark clouds become a furious storm and the child seeks places to hide herself, but eventually she realises she has to find help from a trusted adult.

THE AUTHORSTRATOR

THE BEST PERSON TO ILLUSTRATE A CHILDREN'S PICTURE BOOK IS THE AUTHOR, BUT THERE ARE NOT A LOT OF AUTHORS WHO ARE ALSO ARTISTS.

When an illustrator reads a picture book manuscript they will 'see' the pictures in their mind, and some illustrators are also able to write their own picture book stories. The author-illustrator, or authorstrator, is the ideal picture book creator because their pictures will always be exactly how the author has imagined everything.

However, when submitting a picture book as an authorstrator to a publisher, it's best to send the written manuscript first with maybe one or two final illustrations. Follow up with your dummy book, if and when it is requested. Most publishers like to select their own illustrators to match with a picture book text.

Authorstrator Nicki Greenberg explains her method of pitching her work to her chosen children's publisher:

> When pitching a picture book as an author/illustrator, I provide a brief cover note summarising the format, audience, style, key characters and themes, followed by the complete text of the story broken into paragraphs or stanzas.
>
> I don't indicate which words go on which page, as this is a tricky process that comes later as part of planning the illustrations. The final component is a character sketch or two.

Some authorstrators do not work in two separate stages, such as writing first, followed by the illustrations. Characters may arrive even before the story has become properly formed in their mind, and sometimes the words may even arrive after the images have been created.

Authorstrator Heidi Cooper Smith has worked in this way with the creation of some of her picture books, as in *Six Sleepy Mice* (2019), *Too Many Ducks* (2021) and *Odd Sock Sid* (2022), published by Little Pink Dog Books:

> I started illustrating when I joined an online weekly challenge. Each prompt sparked an idea for a character and, as the character took shape, so did the story behind it. The prompt 'leaves' inspired *Six Sleepy Mice* who were hiding in a deep pile of leaves. 'Octopus' gave life to *Odd Sock Sid*, plagued by nightmares about his overflowing odd sock drawer, and 'bath time' brought to mind a tub full of friendly ducks outstaying their welcome in *Too Many Ducks*.
>
> Although this isn't always how my stories come about, I feel the best illustrations always have great stories behind them. If I were to offer a piece of advice to an aspiring illustrator, it would be to play. Give yourself time to develop your own amazing style and allow yourself to create some truly terrible illustrations along the way!

Many authorstrators who create images before the words are written are outstanding storytellers, and Shaun Tan is one of those amazingly talented and popular authorstrators. Shaun shares his thoughts on visualisation and how pictures fill the gaps in the written narrative:

> Great illustration is not actually illustration. It's storytelling that happens to use pictures instead of words. In the best picture books, the images show us some aspect of the narrative that the words are not telling us, sometimes even a completely different narrative altogether. Often, it's this gap between words and images that most fires up the reader's imagination, not their confluence or descriptive detail. They are like two charged ends of a battery that call upon a reader's personal imagination, memory and instinct to complete the circuit.

cramped
and crowded,

splashed
and splattered...

STEPS IN ILLUSTRATING A PICTURE BOOK

1. CHARACTER DEVELOPMENT

In a visual narrative, such as a picture book, it is so important to have believable characters who are exciting and able to captivate the reader's interest right from the beginning. A child's world is constantly bombarded with images from television and computer games, so your picture book character must be distinctive and dynamic.

Creating the characters is my first major job. It's like choosing characters for a play. I get to know them by drawing them over and over till I know them inside out. — **Ann James**

Your sketchbook is the place to develop these different characters, and your pages should be bursting with all kinds of ideas for personalities: human, animal or inanimate. These ideas can even be drawn from life and then worked on further by redrawing the characters from different angles, showing distinctive attitudes, emotions, facial expressions and movement.

What sort of clothes, hats or shoes does your character wear? And if your chosen character is an animal, will it be anthropomorphic and wearing clothes, or going au naturel? When you are satisfied with the character you've created, then comes the problem of how to draw them exactly alike in each page sequence throughout the 32 pages of your picture book.

This is where those final character drawings from your sketchbook will be invaluable. Make a series of final art studies of your character in different positions, attitudes, actions and showing different facial expressions. Use these to refer to as you work through each page of the picture book layout.

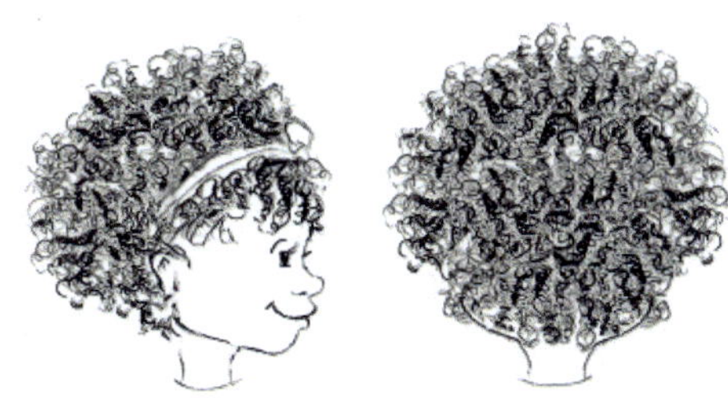

Regarding process, I'm a drawer rather than a painter, so I almost always start with lines. I use two brushes that mimic the look of pencil, and scratch out the picture fairly roughly. When refining the lines, I like to leave some of that roughness — **Simon Howe**

2. THE STORYBOARD

Start with drawing a storyboard template or flat plan, as it is sometimes referred to. Plot how the words and pictures will flow across pages or double-page spreads with your rough thumbnail sketches. It's a little bit like directing a movie as you plan the pace of the drama, action, rhythm, expression, emotion and surprise. Don't get too detailed with these miniature pages; be loose and sketchy as you roughly 'block in' the visual information. As long as you know what's happening in all the boxes, that's all that matters at this stage.

You may find yourself making rather numerous changes to the initial arrangement of your storyboard, so it is helpful to make photocopies to allow for this. Fitting in both text and illustration smoothly and artistically into a 32-page picture book can be quite a complex task.

Remember: the first three pages are normally used for half-title, copyright and publisher information and title page. These first three pages can be and often are illustrated as part of the whole visual narrative for the story. An excellent example is *Bigger Than Yesterday, Smaller Than Tomorrow* (2018) by Robert Vescio, illustrated by Kathy Creamer and published by Little Pink Dog Books.

If you use mainly double-page spreads, then the illustration will need to be in harmony over the whole spread. Avoid placing any vital details, such as faces or important action, where the two pages fold, otherwise known as the gutter.

Double-page spreads over 28 or 30 pages with text at the top or bottom can become rather flat and boring for the reader. Be inventive with each sequence.

> I remember the words of an illustration lecturer back in my college days who said, 'No matter how bad you think an idea is, get it out on paper. That leaves room for better ideas to flow.' This has stayed with me, and I rarely throw rejected pieces away. You just never know when it might be a modified piece in a future puzzle.
> **— Lesley McGee**

The biggest problem you may have will be placing large portions of text without upsetting the word and picture balance. Try to vary the viewpoint over each page, perhaps by going in close to the action or maybe by pulling away from it. Perhaps have an aerial view, or even one from ground level looking upwards, which can add hugely to the dramatic action. When you're satisfied with your storyboard scheme, use it to refer to while designing your dummy book.

> Creating words and pictures for children is a privilege. Reading your story to them is a joy. As an authorstrator, the picture book journey is a long one, filled with ups and downs and plenty of sideways. But believe in your story, follow your heART and commit to the journey, as it is so worth it when you hold your book in your hands! **— Dr Sue Pillans (aka Dr Suzie Starfish)**

STORYBOARD: ***Roger the wrasse and the itchy fishes***

stretch him out or move away from gutter

Move his face further over a little to P14

COPYRIGHT PAGE

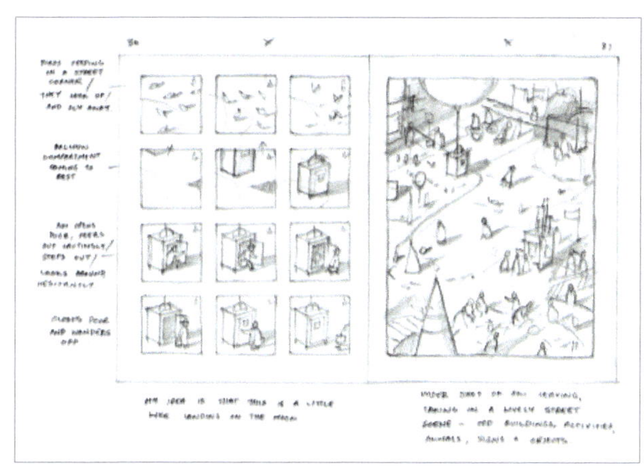

The first stage of the making process for *There's a Tiger Out There* was to create a series of character sketches in pencil. Since I work in collage, I also created a collage version to give the publisher a better idea of how they would finally look. **— Ruth Waters**

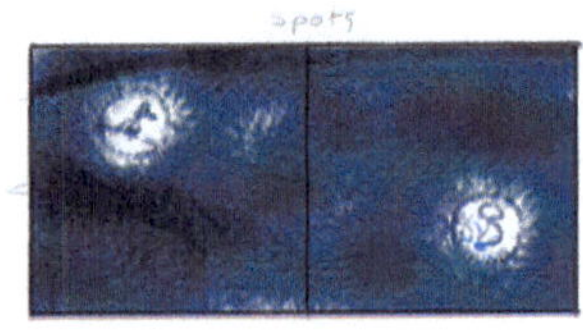

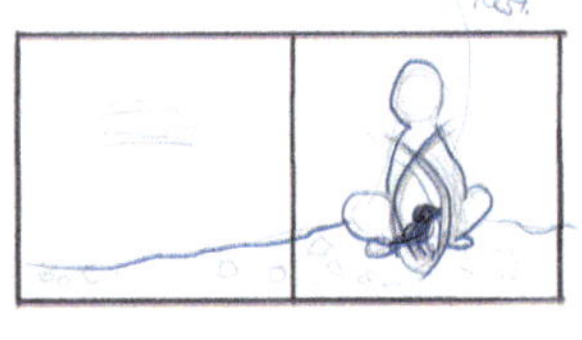

My aim with the storyboard for *Satin*, my forthcoming (2023, MidnightSun Publishing) picture book with Sophie Masson, was to create a shorthand for the shape, colour and flow of the book. Some of the final illustrations are completely different to the storyboard concept, but having that framework lets me make changes while still keeping the bones of the visual narrative intact. Don't worry if your sketches are rough. They are there to get ideas across. It's not like your storyboard will be published in a book for all to see. Usually :) **— Lorena Carrington**

3. THE DUMMY BOOK

Planning a storyboard and then developing a dummy book is essential to successful picture book creation. The dummy book will help you visualise how your sequential images work over 28 pages, and how well the pacing and drama unfold at each important page turn. Visual pace needs to be carefully considered to maintain the reader's interest in the story. This means the sequential imagery must be varied by showing action from different viewpoints, such as focusing closely for extra drama, pulling out to an aerial view to reveal other elements or other changes in the reader's viewpoint.

You may find that there will be areas where the image sequences jump forward too fast, or where the text weight is too heavy, or there are areas where the action or surprise element doesn't work, even with a page turn.

To make your dummy book, you will need eight sheets of paper. Staple them in the middle, then fold them in half to make a 32-page booklet. The dummy is for you to get a feel of your picture book. Use it to see how your visual storytelling will appear over the pages and where the pace of the drama works at a page turn – or doesn't.

You may end up making quite a few different book dummies as you develop your sequential images: you will be moving around the text, cutting out pages, sticking in others and making notes until you are satisfied with the result. Look at your dummy picture book as if you are the child reader and allow yourself to make spontaneous changes.

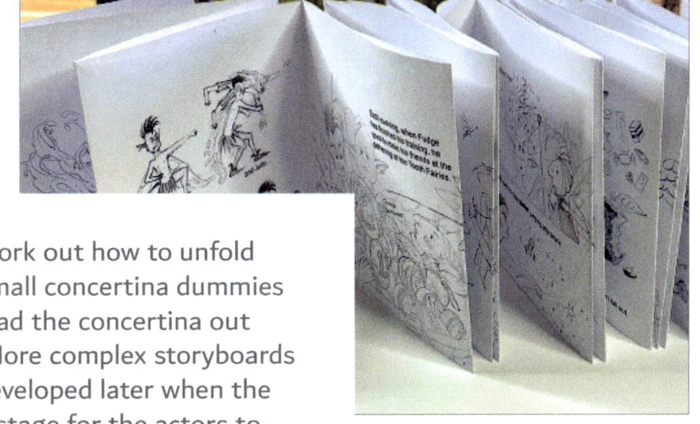

The planning and creation of storyboards and dummy books are such exciting stages of picture book creation, as it's an area where the illustrator can have great fun experimenting with their images and design layout.
— **Kathy Creamer**

Pace in storytelling is so important. To work out how to unfold the story at just the right pace, I make small concertina dummies where I can turn the pages. You can spread the concertina out flat to see the whole story in a stretch. More complex storyboards and dummies with visual detail can be developed later when the 'pagination' is really working. This is the stage for the actors to move across and in-and-out of the pages. — **Ann James**

Lucky's
When it was time for Lucky's race, Mitch led her out to join other racehorses trotting around the enclosure. That was when saw the shoes. Beautiful, fashionable high-heel shoes.
'I'd love to wear shoes like those ones,' she whispered to Mitch. 'Would you fetch me some, please?'
'No,' said Mitch, 'your own lucky horseshoes are the best ones for running races.'
10
11

into the night, carrying
gnashers?
"Oh, no,"
"Now wha

22
move across
Bigger image
END PAPER 2
The BIG OLD RAMBUTAN TREE
Title Page 1
1
...and how to open the prickly shell of the rambutan fruit.
15

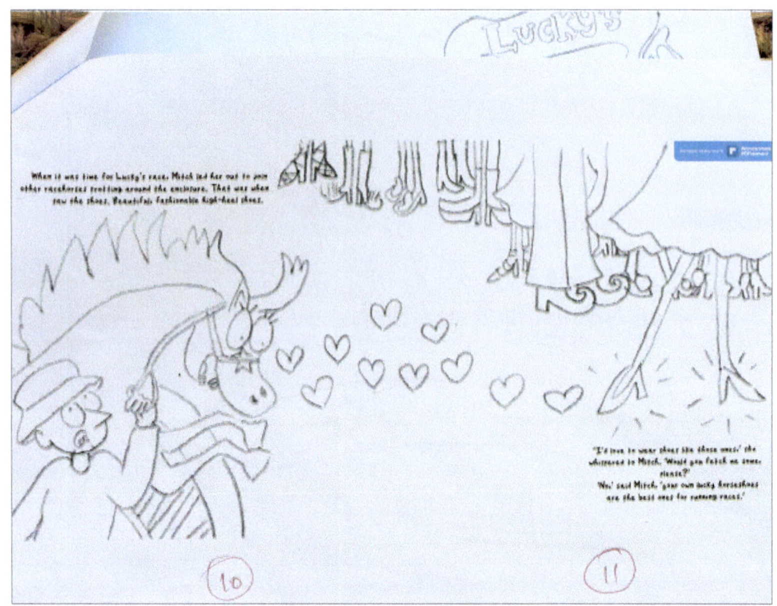

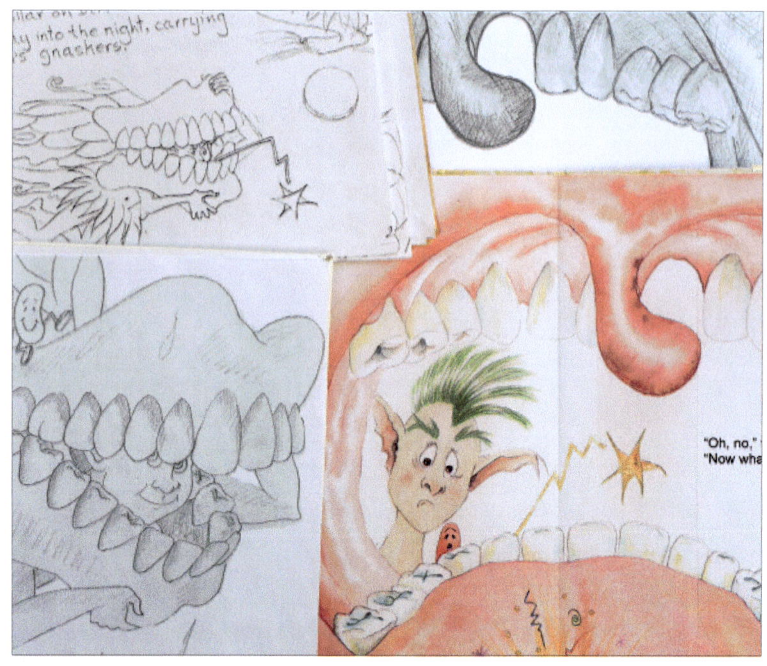

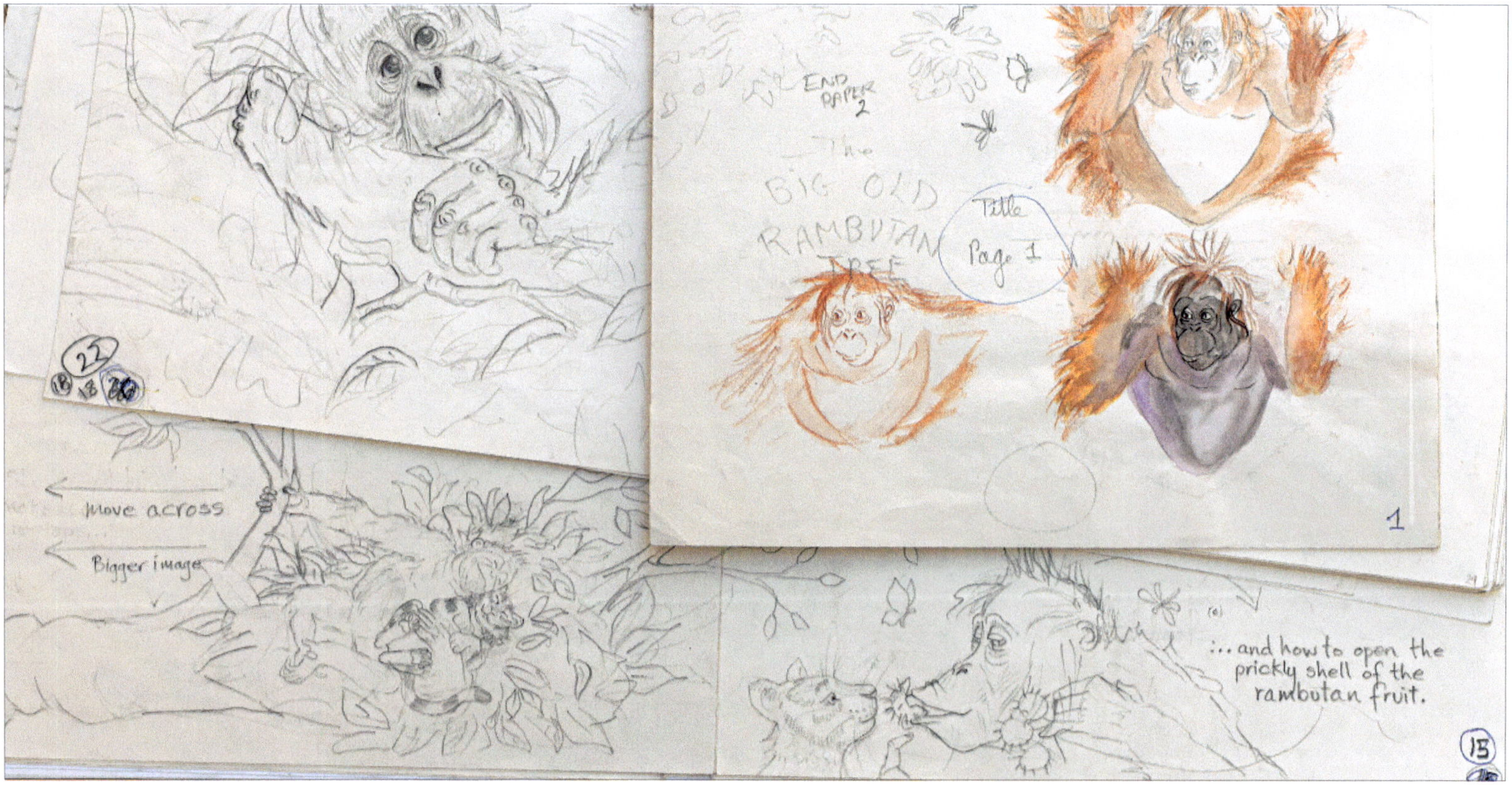

4. FINAL PICTURE BOOK DUMMY

When you're ready to make your final dummy book, it is important that you make it in the proposed size, shape and orientation of your picture book.

Include two or three final illustrations with all the draft illustrations and text in position. Once you've completed your creation, it is time to review the work once again.

ASK YOURSELF:

- Do the words and pictures work together?
- Do the words allow space for my illustrations?
- Do the illustrations give enough space for the words?
- Is there a dynamic interplay between the words and pictures?
- Does the pace of the visual narrative run smoothly, or is there an awkwardness in some of the scene changes?
- Is the text a little too crowded on some pages?
- Is there an opportunity for the use of counterpoint in the illustrations?
- After brainstorming, do I need to make any final changes?

Your dummy book will be an important part of your illustration portfolio presentation to a publisher, or agents and publishers at book fairs and conferences, such as the Bologna Children's Book Fair, Frankfurt Book Fair and London Book Fair.

Join online illustration galleries and online illustration discussion groups. Use Instagram, Facebook and Twitter to showcase your artwork and your published children's books. Join the Society of Children's Book Writers and Illustrators, the ASA Style File, Creative Kid's Tales and Illustrators Australia.

Attend and take part in illustration and picture book workshops, festivals, presentations, seminars, competitions and conferences, such as the ones presented by the Children's Book Council of Australia and the children's, young adult and adult stories conferences.

Create a website to showcase your illustrations and artwork and keep it updated as you create new work.

If you can, always get advice from someone who's already had their illustrations published. Join a professional organisation where you can get advice, join in workshops and competitions, and share your portfolio in their online gallery so that potential clients can view your work. **— Kathy Creamer**

Then the fox sang another verse of her song:

Rooster with your golden crest,
You cannot be the very best,
For good plump corn is not for you,
But lowly hens can chew and chew!

At these rude words, the rooster stuck out his chest and his golden crest glowed with anger. 'How dare you say the corn's not for me!' he shouted, furiously, opening the window to tell the fox what was what. Quick as a flash, the fox grabbed him and took off through the wood.

The rooster was even more frightened and his throat was sore but he managed to yell,

The fox, the fox has me in her jaw,
Dear friends, come quick, or all's up for sure!

Luckily for him the cat and the thrush heard him and they raced after the fox, and pecked and bit and scratched her so badly that she ran away moaning.

5. FINAL ARTWORK

Whatever your illustration style, working technique or favourite medium, you will have to consider if your work is suitable for the book you wish to illustrate. Authorstrator Kathy Creamer had this happen with her recent manuscript, *Mr Ming and the Mooncake Dragon* (2021, Little Pink Dog Books). She intended to illustrate the book herself but found the perfect illustrator in Amy Calautti. Amy has a wonderful range of different illustration styles, and Kathy felt that her quirky pen and watercolour style suited the story so much better than her own artwork.

Artists learn by soaking up visual information and taking parts from different sources to make their style. It's a recipe. You don't have to be pigeonholed into one style; you can play around and keep developing as an artist if you want to. I've experimented with different styles, and I had three different publishers choose a different style for their books. That is how I'm not bound to one approach. Once you've finished refining your drawing and figuring out a style, you then need to learn how to design a page. This takes practice, and I'm always looking for new and interesting ways to lay out a full-page spread.

My basic rules for a page layout are odd numbers of triangles in your composition, a focal point and leading left to right. My advice for aspiring illustrators is to take every opportunity to show your illustrations on social media, whether that be in an illustration group or your own platform. Basically, show everyone. **— Amy Calautti**

I had my setting – a garden. I wanted the book to be full of warm greens, so this environment was perfect. It also allowed me to easily place hints to the final twist! **— Simon Howe**

A StaR for Mama

12
So the next morning the
little pink dog sat outside
in the sunshine all day long.

Little Pink Dog Books
Little Pink Dog Books is based in Armidale, New South Wales, and specialises in high quality children's picture books. Our focus areas as a publisher are:
Animal Conservation
Stories about our wonderful world of wildlife.
Mental Health
Sensitive and funny books to help children deal with everyday fears, anxiety and emotions.
Family
All families are different, and we like to provide warmhearted stories and pictures about family life.
Humour
Laughter is the best medicine! Looking at the funny side of life helps to keep us all happy and healthy.
www.LittlePinkDogBooks.com
refuse
recycle
reduce
reuse
'Less plastic is fantastic'
WHAT DOESN'T BELONG?

Tilly forgets where the house is.
She can't see any lights.
And the sun is setting.
Tilly calls out,
'Cooooeee!
Coooooeee!
Coooeee!'
There's no answer.

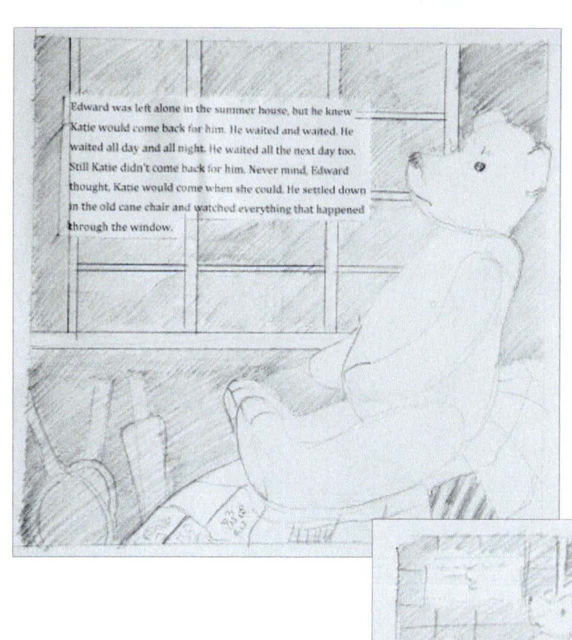
Edward was left alone in the summer house, but he knew Katie would come back for him. He waited and waited. He waited all day and all night. He waited all the next day too. Still Katie didn't come back for him. Never mind, Edward thought, Katie would come when she could. He settled down in the old cane chair and watched everything that happened through the window.

6. THE FRONT COVER DESIGN

In current picture books, the front cover is quite often used as an important part of the narrative, especially when the front cover illustration doesn't duplicate any of the inside pictures. In some picture books, the story can even begin with the front cover and go beyond the last page and onto the back cover, with endpapers included in the narrative. Due to the limited amount of text, even the title itself can convey some of the story.

There are picture books that use a front cover illustration from inside the book itself, which together with the title provides information about the story. Young readers will always choose a book by its cover illustration or its title, so your front covers must be highly attractive and eye-catching.

You shouldn't judge a book by its cover. But whether it's a conscious decision or not, everyone does. — **Beattie Alvarez**

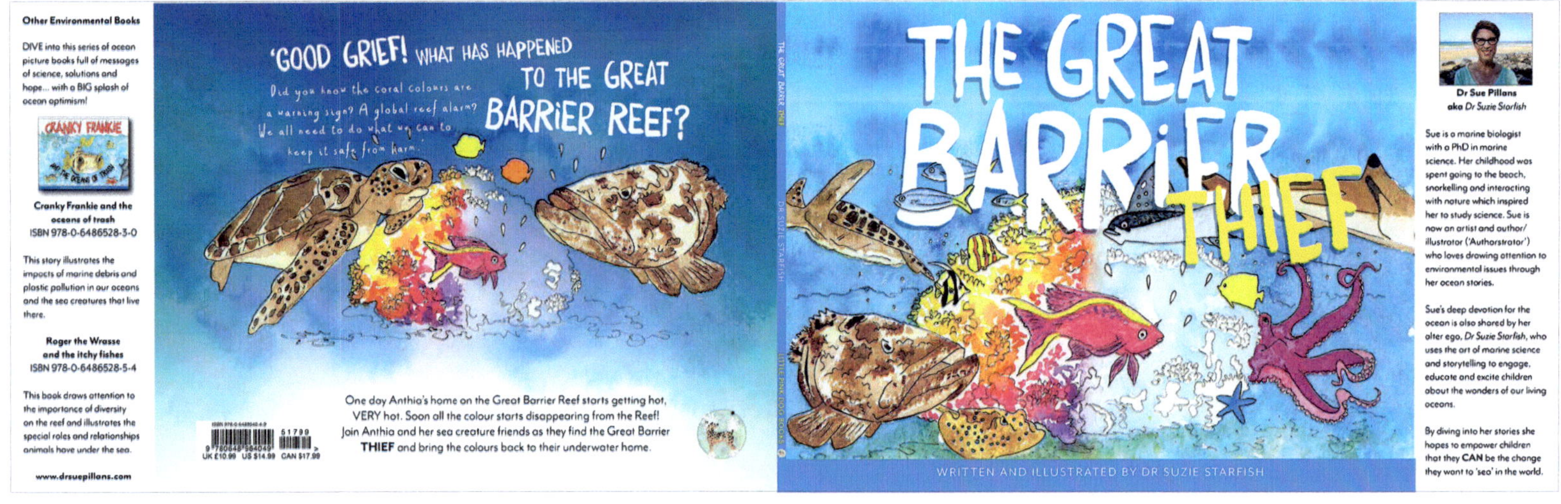

CHECK OUT

Picture book illustrators:

Amy Calautti, Heidi Cooper Smith, Marjorie Crosby-Fairall, Katrin Dreiling, Katrina Fisher, Shiloh Gordon, Jenny Hale, Charmaine Ledden-Lewis, Lesley McGee, Michael McMahon, Emma Middleton, Rebecca Palmer, John Phillips, Heather Potter, Sandra Severgnini, Dr Suzie Starfish, Patricia Ward, Mark Wilson and Julie Vivas.

Authorstrators:

Graeme Base, Mandy Foot, Armin Greder, Roland Harvey, Alison Lester, Shaun Tan and Bruce Whatley.

Using a gatefold on a book cover can enhance the appearance of a book and help to attract more interest. Each fold can be attractively designed to provide additional information about the book, author and illustrator biographies and photographs, explanations about the creation of the illustrations and the illustrator's working methods, advertisements for upcoming books, and details about the publisher.

Advice from authorstrators

New illustrator, Lesley McGee has recently begun her exciting journey towards becoming an authorstrator after having illustrated several books for other authors:

This picture book journey evolved as I began to free my inner visualisation. Artwork is an extension of myself and sometimes difficult to share. Allowing it to run free has brought great joy as words come to life on a page. *The Fabulous Fruit Shake Mystery* (2023, Little Pink Dog Books) began its life without words.

It began with my passion for drawing animals and delicious berries and led to the creation of a series of whimsical artworks. As the characters tumbled out onto my drawing board, it became clearer that their fantastical tale needed to be told and I then began to add the written narrative.

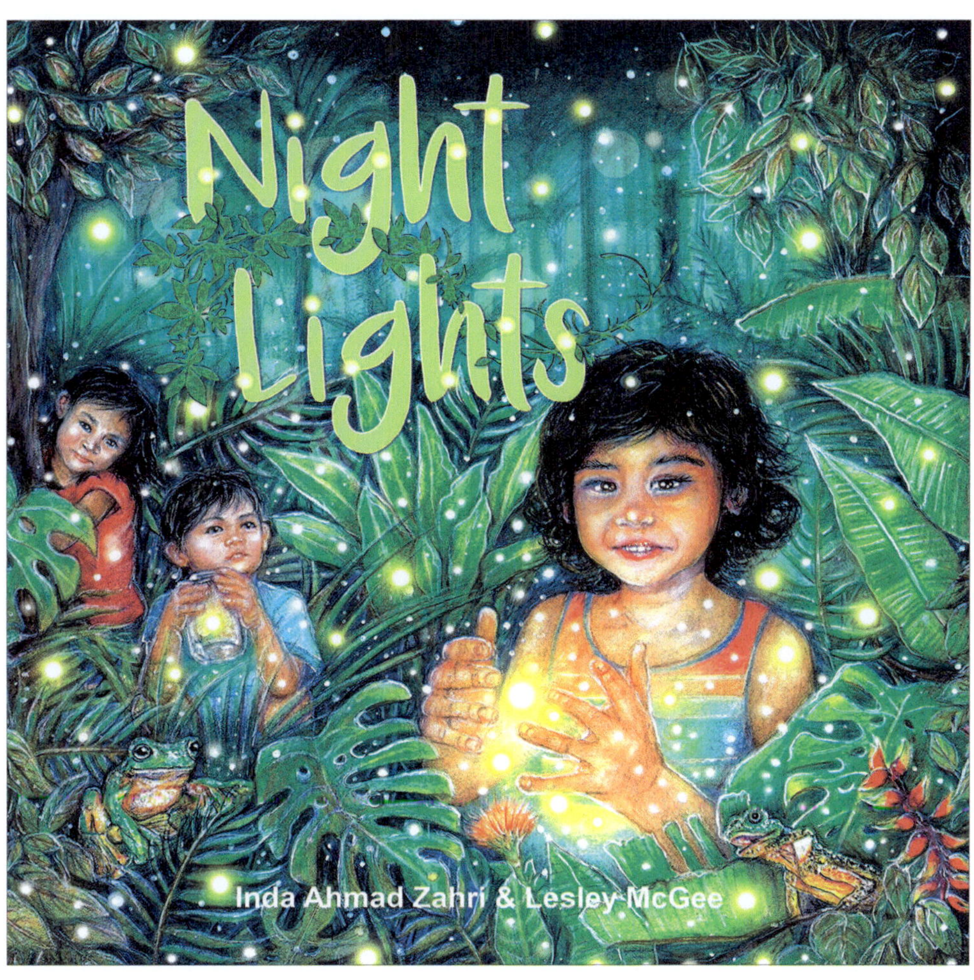

Anne Spudvilas is an authorstrator who makes use of a variety of processes, such as printmaking and collage, to create her beautiful and atmospheric images for her picture books:

In my work, I usually concentrate on depicting the moods and emotions of the characters and how they're feeling about the situation they're in. For my first solo book, *Swan Lake* (2017, A&U Children's), I took the classic ballet story and told it as you would write a ballet program – a brief synopsis of the story told in acts, and each act followed by double-page spreads of illustration with no text at all. I used printmaking, drawing, paint and collage to create the illustrations, which tell the story dramatically in monotones. The lack of colour works well when atmosphere and mood are key elements. Inspiration came from my move up to the Murray River, and I used the riverscape as a reference for the lake, Australian eucalypts and emu feathers as part of the design and our beautiful black swan to create an Australian version of Tchaikovsky's ballet.

Advice from a designer

It is not unusual that sometimes finished artwork for the cover may require more editing on the computer, depending on the situation and story. The artwork can still be rich with detail, but the cover and cover information must have a type of sudden and impactful simplicity for vivid attention. And that can mean a bit more editing, such as the resizing, removal or the covering over of some of the artwork. — **Rae Ainsworth**

Advice from illustrators

As an illustrator of children's and young adult books, I use film and film language a lot in my work. The images must be adding more to the words – either a parallel story or opening out the text in some way.
— Anne Spudvilas

I have always thought of myself as an artist who illustrates books rather than an illustrator, and I think it shows in my illustrations. I approach the work in a more painterly fashion and often think of a style that will fit the story rather than just imposing my illustrative style. Having said that, much of my artwork is full of narrative anyway. As both an artist and illustrator, I think you have much more flexibility if you have some foundation in drawing basics. **— Fiona McDonald**

From the moment I read a manuscript, images appear in my mind. Yet, before I begin illustrating, I have to understand any thoughts the author may have, keeping this in consideration when bringing pencil to page. The next step is research, lots of research, about all facets of the story. Accuracy and detail is a feature of my work, and I am mindful of cultural nuances. My storyboards are a mixture of hand-drawn and digital. Sometimes, the images come so quickly that I can't get them out fast enough. **— Lesley McGee**

I would highly recommend that anyone wishing to illustrate children's books pursue a mentorship through the Australian Society of Authors. I had the pleasure of learning the art of children's books through mentorship with Sue DeGennaro in Melbourne. The industry is daunting for a newcomer, and my mentorship gave me a solid foundation for my career as a children's book illustrator. **— Katrina Fisher**

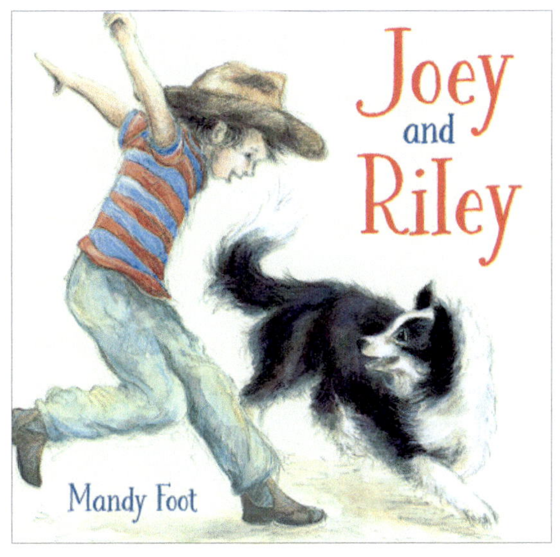

The illustrations in a picture book need to stand alone from the text and vice versa. The biggest compliment an illustrator can receive is for a child to be able to read the book without reading the words. A great manuscript will leave room for the illustrator – combined, they create magic!
— Mandy Foot

ILLUSTRATED STORYBOOKS AND FICTION ANTHOLOGIES

ILLUSTRATED STORYBOOKS

ILLUSTRATIONS FOR STORYBOOKS ENHANCE RATHER THAN EXTEND THE NARRATIVE, WITH THE VISUAL WORLD BEING MUCH LESS EXTENSIVE THAN THAT IN A PICTURE BOOK.

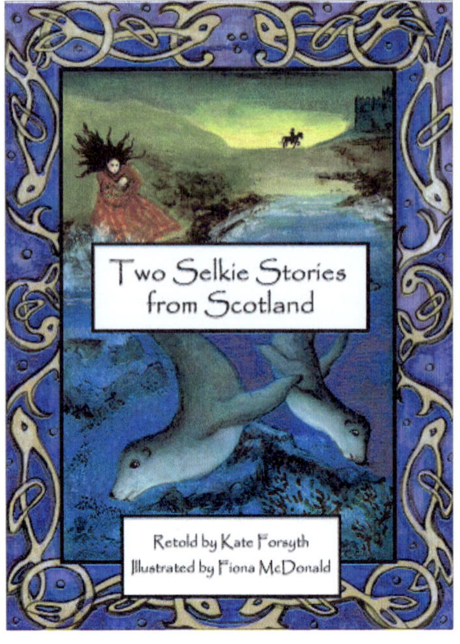

This means the illustrator should take care not to intrude too much into the drama to allow for the reader's imagination. Providing visual prompts to show character, mood and setting will help to stimulate the reader's visual receptiveness and allow them to enjoy the narrative more fully.

Creating illustrations for storybooks for older children can prove to be complicated. The temptation to illustrate areas of text where there is dramatic action may result in repetition of the author's words unless the author has deliberately allowed space for the illustrator to carry the narrative forward.

Another way to illustrate a storybook is to use subtle interpretation by employing a few elements of the drama from the text, such as a ship caught in a storm out at sea, a charging bull, a crushed rose with thorns or a broken pearl necklace. Some illustrators may choose to create decorative emblems and borders utilising certain descriptive elements from the text. This also helps with setting and mood without intruding into the verbal drama.

Illustrator Fiona McDonald uses some of these techniques in her artwork. She describes her way of working and how the inspiration arose with the initial reading of a story where she was to create the visual world.

Kate Forsyth's text for *Two Selkie Tales from Scotland* (2014) published by Christmas Press, really struck a deep, resonating chord with me. I was expecting to enjoy the stories because I enjoy Kate's writing, and I feel very strongly about my Scottish heritage. However, I wasn't expecting the wealth of visual images that bombarded my brain as I read the text. Many of the pictures I did for the book leapt into my mind almost fully formed, including the one of the selkie maiden standing on a lonely beach gazing out to sea. In my mind's eye, I could feel the cold wind, smell the salt tang and hear the dark sea murmuring in its depths.

I wanted to use a painterly style rather than something more traditionally illustrational, such as pen and watercolour wash, and I opted for gouache and acrylic, sometimes using it opaquely and sometimes using it more translucently for painting the water. I decided to do some decorative borders imitating a carved Celtic knot image. This had stylised seals interwoven with scrolls. I also did one of seashells and bits of seaweed to give variety.

For the illustrations in *Two Tengu Tales from Japan* (2015) a retelling by Duncan Ball and published by Christmas Press, the illustrator David Allan also used selected elements from the story to frame the text. Illustrations were used to reveal the setting and character, and double-page spreads were included to show visual drama that isn't revealed in the text.

With *Two Tengu Tales from Japan*, I spent a long time researching traditional Japanese illustrations and art. I wanted it to have an authentic feel that would also be bright and appealing to a younger audience. I sketched out ideas and tried different colour palettes to make sure that I got it right, including the correct clothing and architecture for the period.

I'm a methodical illustrator. I like to take my time researching and sketching before starting a full illustration for a book. The first step is to read the text and work out what needs to be illustrated. Am I illustrating a piece of the text, or am I drawing what isn't mentioned in it?

For the storybook *Three Dragons for Christmas* (2015) – written by Sophie Masson, Fiona McDonald and Beattie Alvarez and published by Christmas Press – illustrator Lisa Stewart describes her way of working on Sophie's story, *The Christmas Dragon*.

> First, I receive the words and begin to scribble down thoughts. Then, I begin character sketches and play around with the character's gestures. I like to try out various watercolour paper thicknesses, and, with the coloured character of Fiery the little dragon, I have used tissue paper, gold leaf, gold gouache, tiny pieces of paper, paint and pencil.

There are other illustrated storybooks for much younger children to share with an adult reader. For this age group, the illustrations must share some of the drama of the narrative as younger children need help to develop their imagination, and they enjoy the repetition of both words and pictures. Children also need to see and understand the facial expression and body language of the characters in the story to feel empathy, understand cause and effect, and begin to develop their emotional intelligence.

One example, as mentioned in the Writing section, is *Hector and his Highland Dancers* by successful writer and illustrator team Anthony Sevil and Amy Calautti.

Looking at the pictures, younger children will learn about Hector's feisty character through his facial expressions, movements, actions and body language.

The text cannot show Hector's character without using lengthy descriptions, so the pictures help the child to visualise Hector. Although the words can describe an action for a child to imagine, the child will want to see and savour, such as the part where Hector pecks a judge's nose! With the words read by the adult, the child will be able to follow the narrative and understand how the picture sequences work in giving more depth to the story. They may also enjoy picking out recognisable words from the text.

FICTION ANTHOLOGIES

MANY ANTHOLOGIES HAVE A SINGLE ILLUSTRATOR TO CREATE THE IMAGES EVOKED BY THE STORIES, BUT OTHERS FEATURE A SELECTION OF DIFFERENT ILLUSTRATORS TO BRING A VARIETY OF COLOURFUL STYLES TO A BOOK OF COLLECTED SHORT STORIES.

Illustrations for anthologies are usually commissioned directly by the publisher, working with illustrators they already know, but there are opportunities for new and emerging illustrators as well. Sometimes there may be a public call for submissions, or an illustrator may be invited to contribute if the publisher has seen their work (for instance, on social media, such as Instagram, or sites like the ASA's Style File and SCBWI's Illustrator Showcase).

If you are invited to contribute to an anthology as an illustrator, the publisher will then allocate you to a story, or stories, depending on how many illustrators are involved. The manuscript will then be sent to you for decisions about what you want to illustrate. The publisher will also brief you on the number of illustrations they require (usually not more than a couple per story, and sometimes just one) and whether they want colour, black and white, or both. They will also let you know the trim size of the book and what bleed to allow for so that you can tailor your illustration to the required format.

It's usual to be paid a flat fee for anthology illustrations, but if you are providing illustrations for a whole anthology, you might be offered a share of royalties as well. Very occasionally, you may not be paid. For the *Kids' Night In* anthologies (2003–2005), which were published to benefit the charity War Child, authors and illustrators donated their work.

Christmas Press featured many different illustrators, from the emerging to the established, in their series of Christmas-themed anthologies (2014–2019). For some books, contributions were invited directly from illustrators, while for others, contributors were chosen from a pool of open submissions depicting a Christmas scene. Illustrators were then matched with stories that the publishers

felt suited their style, but they were free to interpret the story and to use whatever medium they chose.

For example, in *A Miniature Christmas*, Amy Golbach was asked to illustrate two stories: George Ivanoff's 'The Christmas Trap' and Oliver Phommavanh's 'The Funactor'. Both are humorous fantasy stories set in contemporary times but with a different feel. Amy digitally created two illustrations for each story, concentrating on snapshot scenes and sharply defined characters with a different style.

For the same anthology, Kathy Creamer created illustrations for two stories: Stephen Hart's 'The Vaswe Elves', and her own story, 'Christmas with the Fuchsia Fairies'. However, she used very different mediums for these. Her illustrations for 'The Vaswe Elves' were watercolour illustrations, while the illustrations for 'Christmas with the Fuchsia Fairies' were photographs.

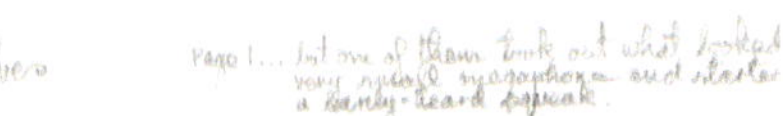

GRAPHIC NOVELS

GRAPHIC NOVELS ARE A DELIGHTFUL WAY FOR WRITERS WHO ARE EXCEPTIONALLY VISUAL TO CREATE AND PRESENT THEIR STORY IDEAS. AUTHORSTRATORS, IN PARTICULAR, MAY HAVE A NATURAL TALENT FOR THIS GENRE.

The graphic novel has grown so much in popularity that over recent years it has even had an influence on the traditional children's picture book, resulting in a kind of genre cross over, with exceptionally beautiful books such as *Cicada* (2018), *The Lost Thing* (2000), and *Rules of Summer* (2013), all by Shaun Tan and published by Hachette. Other popular graphic books for children are Remy Lai's *Fly on the Wall* (2020), published by Macmillan, and *Pawcasso* (2021), published by Allen & Unwin.

The arrangement of limited words, visual narrative and speech bubbles laid out in a series of sequential imagery to convey the drama and action make graphic novels tremendously attractive to those children who are struggling with reading, and especially so for those who may be reluctant readers.

Written and illustrated rather like a film script, the illustrator has to closely follow the writer's art brief for the graphic novel, but they should be allowed to be inventive with their storyboard layout. Both author and illustrator must work closely together and be open to changes as the story develops upon the drawing board.

They both act as movie directors, set designers, costume designers and camera operators.

The written narrative in a graphic novel is usually sparse, with the sequential image and speech bubbles conveying the majority of the storytelling. The dialogue is usually positioned inside speech bubbles of various sizes, taking care not to be too text-heavy, and the narrative is typically placed above or below the dramatic action.

Character, setting and plot in a graphic novel are just as important as in any other genre. They keep to the same structure of an introduction of character and scene, acceleration of action, adventure, climax and the final resolve. Graphic novels are fun to create but can be rather laborious in the design and plotting out of the storyboards, as well as in the creation of the final artwork. David Allan relates the enormous amount of time needed:

> For graphic novels, a fair bit of time is spent storyboarding (sketches in little boxes showing what's happening in each scene). Graphic novels are very time-consuming because you have more illustrations than text and you have to make each box different to the other, even if the characters are still having the same conversation.

The illustrator will have been chosen for their artistic style in order to best enhance the theme, mood and atmosphere of the writer's manuscript. They will follow the art brief and plot their visual storyboard, carefully planning images or frames in a deliberate sequence, together with text, speech, dramatic action, viewpoint and angle.

The writer must not be too rigid in how they 'see' their story, as they do need to allow for the illustrator's own view, imagination and creative design.

Graphic novels allow for a huge range of artistic styles with visual narratives. Most young people are familiar with manga, which is a Japanese style of comic culture, and of course, the extremely popular style of artwork associated with American comic books. Almost any story can be enjoyed as a graphic novel, including fairytales, superhero adventures, horror stories, biographies and even non-fiction.

More challenging is the wordless graphic novel. A magnificent example of this is Shaun Tan's graphic novel *The Arrival* (2006), which has been of exceptional influence in this exciting genre. Shaun Tan's sequential imagery invites the reader into a sepia-tinted and unfamiliar landscape that is sometimes threatening with its depiction of monsters, dragons, peculiar florae, mysterious creatures and bizarre buildings.

It invites the reader to make their interpretation of the visual narrative as they navigate through the events on each page. *The Arrival* provides multiple layers of meaning that encourage the reader to search for signs in image sequences to assist their comprehension of the story.

The Secret Army: Operation Loki (2006) by Sophie Masson and illustrated by Anthony Davis, published by ABC Books, is a graphic adventure with memorable characters and a fast-moving visual narrative.

Anthony's characters are boldly illustrated and his dynamic black and white sequential images are well-paced and action-packed, with the page turns occurring at just the right place to drive the story forwards. This keeps the reader involved and interested in what happens next! Anthony reveals the importance of good illustration:

> Good illustration contains subtle aspects that help convey the emotions and motivation of our character and can drive a story forward visually while complementing the text. The importance of strong posing and good silhouette, and how an image is read by the audience are vital. By taking a good drawing and pushing it a little further, we can improve on this to transform it into a great drawing!

CHECK OUT

The Mediterranean (2017) by Armin Greder is a wordless and moving graphic refugee story, Allen & Unwin; *Fly on the Wall* (2020) by Remy Lai, MacMillan; *Ubby's Underdogs* (2013) by Brenton McKenna, Magabala Books; *Ruben* (2017) by Bruce Whatley, Scholastic Press.

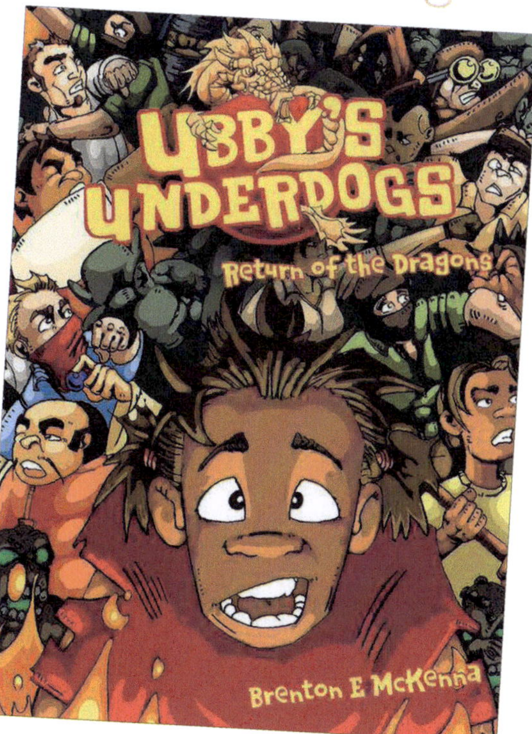

Advice from illustrators

Ho Ho Ho! was my first attempt at creating a graphic-picture book. It is wordless except for the use of a few speech bubbles with the words 'Oh' and 'Ho' throughout the whole of the visual narrative. It was greatly influenced by the imagery in the hugely popular graphic classics, *The Snowman* (1978) and *Father Christmas* (1973), by the renowned UK authorstrator Raymond Briggs and published by Hamish Hamilton. The problem I found with creating the initial layout was how big to draw the images for reproduction. Having never attempted a graphic story before I decided to draw the images the same size as the book size and not reduce them down at all. I drew my frames by hand but then decided to remove them in Photoshop, which helped to give the image sequences cleaner and clearer outlines. A graphic story is extremely time-consuming, and you'll quickly find that you need to work diligently to reach those important time deadlines from the publisher. — **Kathy Creamer**

Creating a graphic novel is like climbing a mountain with six peaks. First there's the manuscript then thumb-nailing, penciling, inking, colouring then lettering. It's a long process so don't forget to pat yourself on the back when you finish each stage. — **Brenton E McKenna**

CHAPTER BOOKS, JUNIOR FICTION AND MIDDLE-GRADE FICTION

CHOOSING WHAT TO ILLUSTRATE IN CHAPTER BOOKS, JUNIOR FICTION AND MIDDLE-GRADE FICTION IS NOT AN EASY PROCESS.

Junior fiction and chapter books are aimed at younger children who are learning to read on their own. They demand a lot from pictures to help children to visualise the action and drama of a story and to help show character and setting. Illustrated chapter books help younger readers to move on up into more complex books, so the illustrator will have to allow for the emerging reader's mind to absorb the words first and then engage with the pictures, which are there to help them appreciate the story and to discover the meanings of new words.

Chapter books, middle-grade and junior fiction aimed at children who are more capable readers will need fewer images to assist them in understanding the story, so the illustrator should only create pictures of certain elements of a story, for example, in *Withering-by-Sea*, written and illustrated by Judith Rossell (2014, HarperCollins).

Judith Rossell's illustrations for her book reveal setting, character, fascinating features and other elements mentioned in her written narrative to heighten the atmosphere of her story, and also to capture the curiosity of the reader. She has avoided illustrating areas where there is high dramatic action in the text, thus allowing for her reader's imagination to visualise this.

Judith describes her processes of working on this book:

> When I started to write *Withering-by-Sea*, I thought of myself as an illustrator who sometimes wrote a bit on the side. I had written a few books, but I was still very anxious and uncertain about writing. I was determined to finish all the words of the story before I started the illustrations because I wanted the story to be able to stand on its own. I pitched the text to HarperCollins without any illustrations.
>
> I loved doing the illustrations. The story is a Victorian melodrama, and I wanted the pictures to help create this mood. I first drew them in pencil and watercolour, then I photocopied them and used watercolour, ink and black Fineliner to add contrast and more details. I really like this effect; the illustrations ended up looking like the engravings in an old textbook. They were dark, formal and a bit overworked, which is exactly what I wanted.

In Sophie Masson's junior fiction story *Four on the Run*, illustrated by Cheryl Orsini (2020, Christmas Press), the illustrations of dramatic action are there deliberately to duplicate the words in order to assist younger readers with their visualisation and to help with their reading comprehension. Using energetic and unpretentious line illustration, Cheryl Orsini's illustrations reveal setting, character, drama and movement. Cheryl describes her working method:

> First, I read the text and start doing very, very rough drawings as the images come to mind. I try to fill every bit of an A4 sheet of paper with these ideas. Then I scan these and in Photoshop, I move them around, re-size them and rotate them, until I feel like the illustration starts to have some balance. Then I print those out and use that as a basis for the rough drawings that I share with the author and publisher. Once the drawings have been approved, I then finish them in readiness for the designer to use in the layout.
>
> For the colour artwork on the cover, I paint every part separately and then I piece it together in Photoshop. I add in a background and some stars, and it's ready to go!

Illustrator Kristin Devine explains her use of a limited visual narrative to reveal character, setting and mood in *Fil and Harry*, written by Jenny Blackford (2021, Christmas Press):

> To illustrate Jenny Blackford's gorgeous manuscript for *Fil and Harry*, I began with several close readings and made simple notes, mind maps and sketches to get a good sense of the main characters, themes and the pacing of the story. I think this is an important step in the process, as it gives you time to explore and develop various ideas before committing to any given one. It can be tempting to jump straight into illustrating, but a little time planning at this stage can save a lot of stress further on!
>
> After developing the appearance of the main characters and selecting which scenes and aspects of the story to illustrate, I was then able to sketch very rough drafts of each scene and make any necessary changes before beginning the final drawings. For *Fil and Harry*, I worked entirely digitally, as it allows me to work quickly and to take more creative risks than I would be willing to take when working on paper or with other traditional mediums.

BLACK AND WHITE

THERE IS A STRONG DEMAND FOR BLACK AND WHITE ILLUSTRATION IN CHAPTER BOOKS, JUNIOR FICTION AND MIDDLE-GRADE BOOKS.

Pen and ink line artwork is much more popular than pen and wash because of the intricate degree of detail, which can be created with crosshatching and the graduated tone this technique can achieve. Fiona McDonald explains her approach to creating her pen and ink illustrations for *Lucy Newton, Little Witch*, written by Phoebe McArthur (2018, Christmas Press):

Pen tends to reproduce better on the types of paper used for chapter books and novels. I was working with Beattie Alvarez on the whole design of the book, and she had some very determined ideas as to how it should look and feel. I was very happy to work with these directions and we corresponded over how things should be. For instance, I did some pencil sketches of the character Lucy. Beattie would suggest they were either too young or too old, the dress needed to be longer, shorter, that kind of thing. When we had the basic look of Lucy right, then I did her in felt-tip art pen. The same process was used to develop Tom, Lucy's black cat, with the one white hair in his tail.

I think the hardest picture of all was Lucy's house. We wanted it to be a bit stylised, like a storybook house. I had trouble trying not to do straight lines. Then we had to draw the slug. I love slugs, especially those big leopard slugs, and I love drawing the slugs doing different things. Beattie asked for a series of different sized slugs to use across the pages. And slugs always leave a slime trail!

FRONT COVERS

FRONT COVERS FOR CHAPTER BOOKS, JUNIOR FICTION AND MIDDLE-GRADE FICTION SHOULD INDICATE WHAT THE STORY IS ABOUT, BUT WITHOUT GIVING AWAY TOO MUCH INFORMATION.

Book covers have to be appealing and sometimes the cover design may not be by the same illustrator who created the inside illustrations, but by a different artist or designer. The need for an eye-catching front cover design is always crucial to promote the book and make it stand out from all the other books in the shop, as explained by Beattie Alvarez:

> Each cover goes through countless variations. It has to relate to the text, be engaging and appealing and be different to other books out there. The right fonts have to be chosen – I choose fun, easy-to-read ones for the chapter books, slightly more sophisticated for the middle-grade, but always ones that 'POP' off the page. The same goes for the colour, bearing in mind that blue can look more like purple in the final print and that pink can be seen as gender bias. The examples of my cover designs show how many versions some have gone through.

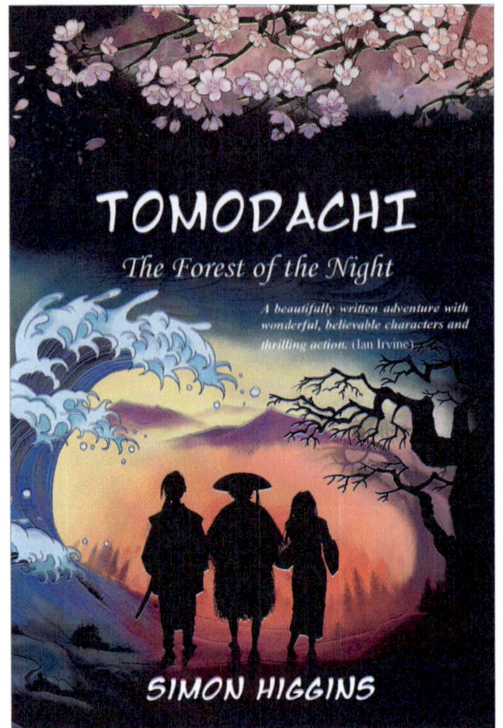

First, I use the logical side of my mind to research the most fitting art medium and analyse the story's content and themes. After that, I let the dreamy side take over and I sketch and play with images until the right design says, 'Here I am!' **— Jenny (Yuxiao) Wang, illustrator of *Tomodachi: The Forest of the Night***

As with all of our covers, *Jules Verne's Mikhail Strogoff* went through several variations before the design team settled on the final cover. The only thing we were sure of was our dislike for classic books with modern covers. We like our covers to fit the style, context and content of the book inside. We decided on a classic look, mimicking the books of old – gold embellishments, inset cover image – but as always, it wasn't that simple. Even picking the colour was hard! Lots of research was done and we agreed that the book needed to be blue. However, as you can see, we went with red in the end, to help it 'pop' on the shelves and giving it a warm and cosy feel, the type of book that you'd curl up with on a rainy day.

When talking about book covers people forget that books actually have a front and a back cover – and each is important, to say nothing of the spine. When the team was designing *Jules Verne's Mikhail Strogoff* we had to keep all of that in mind. Our use of vintage frames on the front cover was repeated on the back and even inside to create a sense of consistency and a nice flow effect, even though they were black instead of gold. **— Beattie Alvarez, designer**

NON-FICTION

CREATING IMAGES FOR NON-FICTION CAN BE ENORMOUS FUN. IT IS CHALLENGING WORK FOR AN ILLUSTRATOR, AS THERE IS USUALLY A GREAT DEAL OF RESEARCH TO DO.

You also need to have the essential technical drawing skills. When presenting factual illustrations, the biggest challenge to the illustrator is to bring learning to life in a creative, visually interesting way that will grasp the reader's attention and imagination. In a world where children are constantly surrounded by moving images through film and television, interactive computer games and virtual reality, the stationary image still has the power to engage. This allows children to enjoy and explore an image without the use of a fast forward button.

Non-fiction can cover areas such as science, history, biology, human biology, geography, visual dictionaries, natural history, counting and alphabet books, and include puzzle books and games. Research is the foundation for illustrating non-fiction; you will need to invest in a large selection of detailed reference books and a good stock of photographs. Publishers will sometimes provide reference materials for specific areas, but you may have to source these for yourself.

Note that some non-fiction doesn't need the detailed illustrations that might be necessary for natural history or science. Illustrators may instead be asked to contribute picture elements that can be repeated or otherwise incorporated into the internal design in a way that helps to break up the text.

This helps to create an appealing and accessible atmosphere for young readers. An example of this is Ursula Dubosarsky's *Word Spy* books, where illustrator Tohby Riddle created a variety of silhouettes and other motifs that highlighted the playful nature of the words. Along with design features such as occasional blocks of colour, it formed an eye-pleasing visual world.

Full-colour, fully illustrated (i.e. not photographic) non-fiction books for children represent a lot of work in regard to both pictures and words. In our Writing section on 'Non-fiction' (page 24), Sami Bayly, award-winning authorstrator of bestselling books, described how research influenced both her illustrations and her words.

Here Sami describes how her illustration process allows her to create a look that works well in the non-fiction genre:

> My preferred medium is watercolour and white gouache. By combining these elements, I can create a realistic finish as well as including my personal style. I begin with a sketch and then move onto a wet-on-wet method, meaning I wet the area first before adding my paint. This allows the pigment to blend and show no signs of brush strokes. I will then move onto a wet-on-dry method, where I will paint onto the dry paper. After numerous layers, I finish the piece with white gouache in areas, such as the glisten in an eye or the shine on a scale.

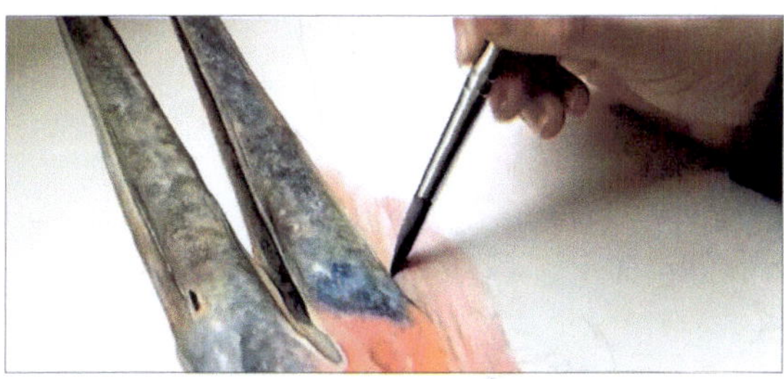

Advice from an authorstrator

Photographic non-fiction books for children are a lot of work and take a lot of time, especially if you are an authorstrator, like Jan Latta, whose internationally popular books about wild animals feature her fantastic photographs. Her central tip for authorstrators who may want to try their hand at creating appealing children's photographic non-fiction is 'make your characters come alive'. Jan describes her painstaking process:

> First, I do research. This may take months or sometimes years because I need to know everything about a wild animal to keep myself safe. Then I travel to the country to find the animal, hire a guide and follow animals in the wild to tell their story through photographs. I decided against illustrations because I wanted to create a 'real' true to life book. I always write an outline of the story, which is my wish list of action photographs I hope to be able to take in the animal's natural habitat. Sometimes the animals rewrite the story when I'm close to them and that is special. Back in my studio, I edit the photographs and write the text.

CHECK OUT

Books by Sami Bayly: *The Illustrated Encyclopedia of Ugly Animals* (2019), *The Illustrated Encyclopedia of Dangerous Animals* (2020) and *The Illustrated Encyclopedia of Peculiar Pairs in Nature* (2021), all published by Hachette Australia.

Books written by Ursula Dubosarsky and illustrated by Tohby Riddle: *The Word Spy* (2007), *The Word Snoop* (2009) and *The Return of the Word Spy* (2013), all published by Penguin.

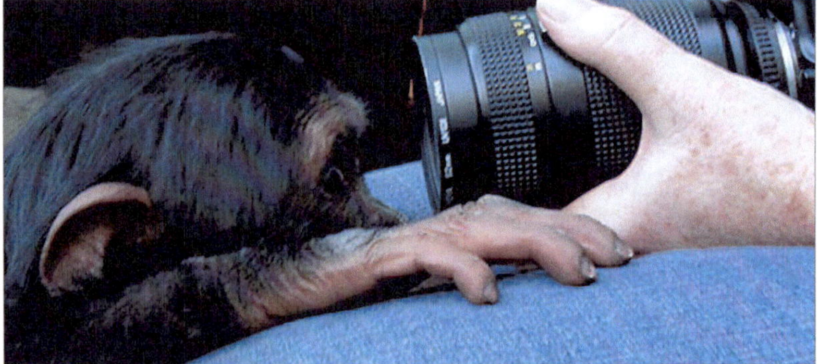

POETRY

POETRY CAN BE A DIFFICULT GENRE FOR ILLUSTRATORS. THE POEMS THEMSELVES ARE PAINTING PICTURES WITH WORDS, AND THE ILLUSTRATION CAN OFTEN JUST BE REPRODUCING THE TEXTUAL IMAGERIES IF IT TAKES A TOO LITERAL METHOD.

A more successful approach to creating pictures for poetry is for the illustrator to be allowed to have a totally personal response to creating the artwork, and this will sometimes result in a beautiful contrast or even counterpoint with the text.

Poetry for young children is less challenging for an illustrator as it does allow for that literal approach to help with visualisation for the child reader, especially with comic verse, such as nonsense rhymes. It gives delicious freedom for a dancing, playful and idiosyncratic style of illustration.

Poetry collections and anthologies for children are always illustrated, usually by one person. However, the recent poetry anthology *A Boat of Stars* went a different path by featuring the work of many different illustrators as well as many different writers. The result is a great diversity in its visual world and its written one, but also a beautiful sense of coherence and unity.

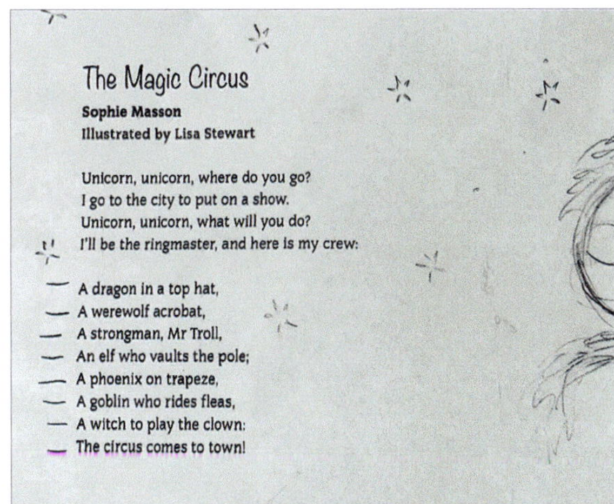

The Magic Circus

Sophie Masson

Illustrated by Lisa Stewart

Unicorn, unicorn, where do you go?
I go to the city to put on a show.
Unicorn, unicorn, what will you do?
I'll be the ringmaster, and here is my crew:

A dragon in a top hat,
A werewolf acrobat,
A strongman, Mr Troll,
An elf who vaults the pole;
A phoenix on trapeze,
A goblin who rides fleas,
A witch to play the clown:
The circus comes to town!

Illustrators were free to interpret poems as they wished, as Lisa Stewart describes when it came to her creation of the illustrations for Sophie Masson's poem, 'The Magic Circus':

> Sophie Masson is a prolific and outstanding author, and she's a dream to work with. For her poem 'The Magic Circus', the illustration came quickly to my mind. I chose only to do the dragon in a top hat hovering in the sky of stars above the circus tent. Even though more characters are in Sophie's poem, I wanted to let the reader go on their own visual adventure of the circus. I love being an illustrator and being a part of the wonderful world of books. I feel lucky that I get to do so and am inspired by authors and poets.

CHECK OUT

A Boat of Stars (2018) edited by Margaret Connolly and Natalie Jane Prior, ABC Books; *A Pocketful of Rhymes* (2017) written by Max Fatchen and illustrated by Kathy Creamer, Christmas Press; *Join the Armidale Parade!* (2019) written by Sophie Masson and illustrated by Kathy Creamer, Little Pink Dog Books; *The Christmas Garden* (2019) written by Caroline Tuohey and illustrated by Sandra Severgnini, Little Pink Dog Books; *The ABC Book of Australian Poetry* (2010) written by Libby Hathorn and illustrated by Cassandra Allen, HarperCollins.

Footnote

Young Eric's socks are getting stronger,
And if he wears them any longer,
Then we can only hope and pray
The breeze will blow the other way.

Advice from an illustrator

For *A Pocketful of Rhymes*, I read each poem carefully and tried to pick out elements of the imagery without giving away what each poem was about. I used black line and wash with small amounts of crosshatching for texture, and I concentrated on conveying movement, action and humour. — **Kathy Creamer**

PLAYS

PLAYS FOR CHILDREN CAN BE INTERESTING TO ILLUSTRATE, EVEN IF IT'S NOT A COMMON MEDIUM TO WORK WITHIN.

Individual plays are often published in *The School Magazine*, with illustrations in colour or black and white, and it's worth having a look at editions of the magazine to research the aesthetic. When it comes to books, however, black and white illustrations are the norm; check out the plays listed below. Illustrators will be briefed by the publisher on the stories and characters of the plays, but it's a good idea to read each play for yourself to decide what scene or characters you'd most like to illustrate. Remember that plays are meant to be performed as well as read, but they are always going to be read first, so first impressions are important and that includes any illustrations. As there are only a few illustrations in a book of plays, it's important to 'set the scene', so think about how you can emphasise an aspect of a character or a scene. For example, in *The Boy Who Could Fly*, there is only one illustration per play, always at the beginning.

In 2016, Duncan Ball wrote a brand-new additional play, 'The Teeth of a Vampire', for his collection *This School is Driving Me Nuts and Other Funny Plays for Children*. Publisher Christmas Press commissioned the original illustrator, Craig Smith, to create a few extra illustrations that would feel like part of the same visual world as the rest of the book. After reading the new play, Craig came up with some illustrations that perfectly conveyed the zany humour of the play – with a slightly creepy edge! (See some of Craig's illustrations on page 28).

CHECK OUT

This School is Driving Me Nuts and Other Funny Plays for Kids (1988, revised 2016) written by Duncan Ball and illustrated by Craig Smith, Christmas Press; *The Boy Who Could Fly and Other Magical Plays for Children* (2019) written by Ursula Dubosarsky and illustrated by Amy Golbach, Christmas Press.

I enjoy using pose and expression to communicate a character's personality, employing a gentle sort of humour. — **Amy Golbach**

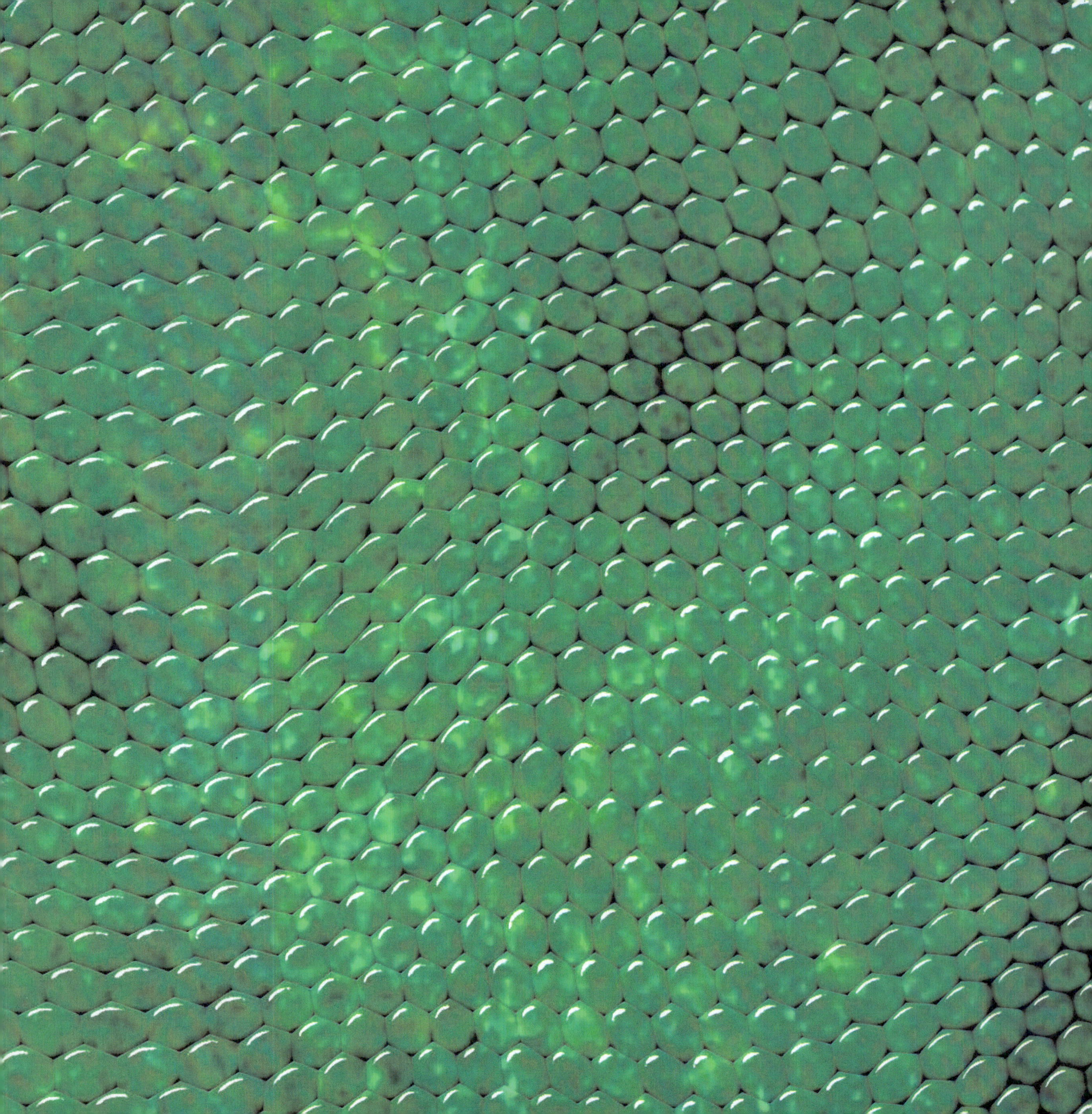

PUBLISHING

LITERARY AGENTS

THE MAIN PART OF A LITERARY AGENT'S JOB IS TO SECURE PUBLISHERS FOR THE WORK OF THE WRITERS AND ILLUSTRATORS THEY REPRESENT.

They send their clients' work to publishers, negotiate publishing deals, check and negotiate contracts, examine sales and royalty statements, and make sure their clients are offered as many opportunities as possible, including potential speaking engagements. They may also negotiate film and other subsidiary rights, depending on the type of contract their clients have with publishers. Additionally, they are often the first readers of a manuscript, especially for new authors, and may give advice and feedback in order for it to be in the best shape to send to a publisher. Agents cultivate good relationships with their clients but also with a wide range of publishers and other publishing professionals. This means contact through phone, email and meetings, in person or online, making an agent's day very busy indeed.

For all of this work – good agents do a lot for their clients – they are paid a commission of around 15 per cent, which is deducted from the earnings of a book. Deductions can include 15 per cent of an advance, royalties or lending right payments (if the agent handles those).

Most reputable agents do not charge any upfront fees, registration fees or reading fees. That is certainly the case with members of the Australian Literary Agents' Association (ALAA) www.austlitagentsassoc.com. There are many advantages to having an agent:

- Your work is never classified as 'unsolicited', and it does not go on 'the slush pile', because of the relationships a recognised agent has cultivated in publishing.
- You do not have to deal with the sometimes thorny business of checking and negotiating contracts and deals, as they will do that for you.
- You can talk over creative and publishing issues with, and get advice from, a trusted professional who can supervise your legal and financial interests in publishing.

However, not all established writers and illustrators have agents, and it's not always easy – though certainly not impossible – for a new, unpublished creator to secure an agent's representation.

To have the best chance of doing so, make sure you do your research and approach an agent who handles children's book creators, for instance, look up the ALAA website, as noted above. Follow their submission guidelines, just as you would for a publisher, and make sure your work is in the best possible shape for presentation.

Be sure to pitch yourself as someone they can represent long term, not just for one book. Of course, respect and courtesy must always be to the fore!

Advice from an Agent

What I look for in a manuscript is a great story. I might love the characters or the beautiful writing, but the story is what makes me disappear into the world. And what I look for in an author, after finding a great manuscript, is someone who understands publishing is a business and approaches it with fun, passion and commitment. — **Alexandra Adsett, principal at Alex Adsett Literary Agency**

PUBLISHER AND PUBLISHING DIRECTOR

THE TITLES ‘PUBLISHING DIRECTOR’ AND ‘PUBLISHER’ ARE OFTEN USED INTERCHANGEABLY, BUT THEY MAY OCCASIONALLY DENOTE A SLIGHTLY DIFFERENT ROLE.

In medium or large companies, ‘publishing director’ will often indicate an overview position across a range of divisions or departments, while ‘publisher’ will often have a descriptive tag attached to it, such as ‘Publisher, Children’s Books,’ indicating the person oversees a particular division. In bigger companies, several publishers and publishing directors report to an overall managing director. However, in small presses, where people wear many hats, ‘publisher’ and ‘publishing director’ often mean the same thing – it’s up to the company to decide the term. Due to limited size, there isn’t usually a separate managing director, although some companies, especially non-profit ones, have a board.

The publisher or publishing director may have commissioning editors reporting to them on potential acquisitions, but they could also directly select books for acquisition meetings themselves. In small companies, they will have the final say on what is published, and in bigger companies, they will be a central part of the decision process, perhaps with other senior staff.

Publishers and publishing directors alike determine the shape and feel of their publishing lists in consultation with other staff. They may also initiate new lists and have a sense of how some might develop in the future. They will oversee editorial, design and production teams, and in small presses, will be very hands-on regarding production. They will often seek out illustrators and keep an active list in their databases.

The publisher or publishing director is at the end of a long chain when a book is acquired, especially in larger and medium companies. When a proposal or submission by a writer is sent to a publishing company, it usually goes first to the submissions team, and if deemed worthwhile, it will be passed onto the editorial team. If there is one, the commissioning editor will receive the work next and discuss it with the publisher.

As publishers, we are committed to broadening the range of children’s picture books for all children. I personally find working to help new and emerging authors and illustrators enter the children’s picture book industry a very fulfilling endeavour. **— Peter Creamer, publisher, Little Pink Dog Books**

In a small press, the process will be similar, but there will be much fewer staff along the way – in some cases, only two or three. It is slightly different for illustrators, who may be approached directly by publishers or who may submit portfolios, which will be passed to the publisher for review to decide whether that illustrator could be added to their active list.

Note that in all companies, the publisher or publishing director is not your first port of call when submitting a manuscript. Don't address queries or cover letters to them, but rather to the commissioning editor (if there is one) or simply to an editor. If you know the name of that person, use that, but 'Dear Editor' will be sufficient. If your pitch is successful, then further down the track, especially in small companies, you may be in touch with the publisher.

In larger companies, it will often be the commissioning editors and other editors who correspond directly with you all the way along. Nevertheless, it is useful for authors to have an understanding of the role of the publisher and publishing director and to research the ways that people in those roles in publishing companies see the shape and future of their lists.

Cathi Lewis, publisher Wild Dingo Press, on devising a new list:

I come from an educational background, so I am passionate about inspiring young people to engage with books. I developed the concept of the *Aussie STEM Stars* series to introduce young readers to our many world-leading scientists and their inventions. The aim was to celebrate these 'STEM Stars' and to show young readers that, in many cases, these scientists had navigated significant hurdles in their lives. In fact, during school, they weren't necessarily excellent at the subject they became experts in, but with resilience and hard work, they achieved amazing results.

The stories also show how STEM subjects can lead to all sorts of careers that students of this age group (from 10 to 13 years) may never have imagined. We did our market research by looking at the fiction and non-fiction for the age range and discussing the concept with school librarians, booksellers and children.

COMMISSIONING EDITOR

WHAT IS A COMMISSIONING EDITOR? THE SHORT ANSWER IS THEY ARE THE ONES WHO CHOOSE WHAT BOOKS TO PUBLISH.

The long answer is they are the gatekeeper and your entry into publishing. Particularly with smaller publishers, their inbox receives your submissions and proposals; therefore, your work has to be as polished as possible. If you don't impress the commissioning editor, then you aren't published. They choose the best manuscripts and convince the publishers or publishing directors (who have the final say) that certain books should be published. Sometimes they also devise ideas for books and find authors to write them. Commissioning editors are generally the ones who manage contracted book schedules, ensuring the manuscript is delivered by the due date, editing is done and illustrations come in promptly. In many small publishing houses, the commissioning editor may also be the copyeditor, proofreader and designer of the books.

An ordinary working day – according to a commissioning editor at a small publisher who wishes to stay anonymous to avoid an influx of unsolicited submissions – starts with a coffee.

If they're on a deadline for publication, they prepare the files for printing. This can involve creating the full design of a book, dropping the text into the program, ensuring illustration colours are correct, editing, proofreading and making sure the page numbers line up. If it's a slow day, they will read any solicited submissions to search for potential publications.

Often, there are talks with the head of the publishing company regarding projects (upcoming books, publicity and talks about submissions) and goals for the next two or even three years of the company. When discussing submissions, there are two types frequently encountered in the publishing industry. Unsolicited submissions are manuscripts that have been sent to a publisher who didn't ask for them and, in all probability, doesn't want them.

Solicited submissions, however, are sent through a literary agent by request of the publisher or during an open submission period, which for most publishers is at least once a year.

> The difference between the two is quite possibly the difference between getting published and finishing up on the slush pile or worse – blacklisted.
>
> Commissioning editors need to know that the author is going to be easy to work with.

One very simple test is can you follow guidelines and rules? If you can't, then how can the commissioning editor be sure that you will get the work done on time or accept editing suggestions?

EDITORS

EDITORS PLAY A VERY IMPORTANT ROLE IN THE DEVELOPMENT OF A PUBLISHED BOOK. THEY READ, REVIEW AND IMPROVE WRITTEN CONTENT, WHETHER THAT IS PICTURE BOOK TEXT, FICTION, POETRY, PLAYS OR NON-FICTION.

Once your manuscript has been acquired by the publisher, the editor starts work on it, beginning with a structural (sometimes known as a substantive) edit.

This is where the editor will read the whole manuscript, make comments and notes, and look to make sure the structure of the book works. They may examine such things as the plot and if there's continuity in action and characters, for example, with timing or description. They also consider prose style, including errors related to grammar or spelling. The edited manuscript will then be sent to the author for review and revision, often complete with a style sheet to help navigate through the edits. As an author, you don't have to accept all suggestions, but it's wise to look at it properly before you argue, as the editor's job is to look with fresh eyes at your manuscript to ensure it works for readers. You may also have revisions of your own, of course. Following the first big edit, there may be a second, smaller structural edit, if it's felt to be necessary.

Once the structural edit is complete, and it is agreed to by the author, then a copy edit will be done, which will look more closely at errors involving grammar, spelling, punctuation, typos, etc. Continuity will also be examined. Sometimes, the same editor will do both the structural and the copy edit; sometimes it will be a different person for each stage. Once again, the copy edit will be sent to the author for review and revision, then go back to the editor for a final check. After the copy edit is completed, it will be time for proofreading. This is when the book has been laid out, and the pages are being checked for any remaining errors and typos that might have slipped through. It's the last stage of editing and may be undertaken by the same editor or a dedicated proofreader (although this is rare these days).

The proof will also be checked by other people in the publishing team, and, of course, by the author. Often there will be a second proof, which will incorporate any corrections made in the first proof. That's the final editing stage before the book goes to the printer.

Professional editors may be employed in-house at a publisher, or they may be freelance and contracted for particular books. Both types of work patterns may occur in publishers of all sizes. Editors may have completed a university degree in editing, or they may have completed shorter courses, such as those organised by the Institute of Professional Editors Limited, or, especially in smaller publishing houses, they may have learned their skills through on-the-job training. In all instances, editing is highly skilled work and requires very particular qualities that aren't just about good reading skills, an ability to spot errors and a good grasp of ways to improve a text.

A good editor also needs patience, imagination, concentration, discretion and excellent communication skills, as they are often the ones dealing most closely with the author.

Working as a professional editor:

Editing children's books is about the journey it takes me on, through the eyes of the child reader. I help writers to present their prose and experience for the child's age. At times, I'm the caretaker for an author's childhood memories, while keeping the audience in mind. It gets tricky when someone sends me their manuscript and says, 'My grandchildren, mum, partner and best friend loved my story. You won't need to change anything!' My role as an editor is to polish and refine the MS, but it can sometimes become quite personal in supporting and encouraging the author.
— Jen Scanlan

Working as a book editor for the first time:

When I was offered an internship at Christmas Press, the task of editing children's books for the first time was intimidating. However, the genre was only minimally different from editing other forms of content, and I found that standard tactics could be used for copyediting and proofreading. The only noticeable changes emerged with the need to check for inappropriate material or obscure content that would be too impenetrable for the target age range. **— Sharnee Rawson**

ART DIRECTOR

THE ART DIRECTOR WITHIN A LARGE CHILDREN'S PUBLISHING HOUSE HAS THE RESPONSIBILITY OF CREATING THE LOOK, STYLE, TONE AND OVERALL DESIGN OF THE BOOKS.

Generally, they work in a team with the editor, graphic designer and illustrator to develop ideas for the publishing company's book list and to determine the best visual style for each book. The art director needs to have good imaginative, artistic and conceptual talents as well as strong communication skills to convey their ideas and inspire their creative team. They manage all the different stages of book production, from the manuscript stage to the final artwork, ready for printing. In addition, they have to be adaptable and make changes to their initial concept if a book is not working for the publishing team.

Small independent publishing houses, such as Little Pink Dog Books, share the role of the art director among the team, from commissioning editor to illustrator, writer and graphic designer. Everyone contributes to the design of the proposed book, with the publisher having the final decision. The commissioning editor and the writer select the best illustrator for the story. The illustrator usually proposes the front cover design, with input from the graphic designer and the commissioning editor. The team must be open about the design, as this will often be suggested by the illustrator's natural style of artwork.

DESIGNERS

DON'T JUDGE A BOOK BY ITS COVER. THAT SAYING SEEMS REASONABLE – IN THEORY. BUT REALISTICALLY, AN ATTRACTIVE, EYE-CATCHING COVER MAKES READERS PICK UP A BOOK IN THE FIRST PLACE.

It is the job of designers to manage visual appearance. There is some crossover between book designers and graphic designers, but with small presses, these are often the same role. It is the designer's job to turn a manuscript into a book. It's more than just making a book look pretty, although that is a big part of the job.

If it's a picture book, the designer must choose the best layout for the illustrations and the words by ensuring they work together on the page for the best reading experience. Even in books without illustrations, there's a lot of work involved. Designers have to select the best margins (where the text starts and ends on ALL sides of the page). If the text is too close to the inside margins, then it will get lost in the crease. Additionally, if the text is too far towards the bottom, the reader's thumbs will cover the words when holding the book. The designer also has to select fonts and decide how the chapter titles look. They must take care with the placement on the page and make sure the font suits the story while still being easily readable.

Generally, a designer will develop a concept, or several concepts, and do a few sample pages before sending it for approval to the publisher or author (depending on whether it's traditionally published or self-published). Once that is approved, they continue with the final product. The same goes for the cover of a book. The designer has to choose the font and word placement carefully. They ensure the text and the image work coherently to make the cover as appealing as possible.

A designer's contribution:

I love it when an illustrator brings me in to talk over their work and thoughts regarding the illustrations. This also applies to their interactions with words in a storyboard or proposed layout. It doesn't always happen, and it doesn't have to. Each book and publishing group has a preference and an experience for how things work smoothly. I don't have to own every aspect of a project to enjoy contributing what I can.
— Rae Ainsworth, designer

From idea to printed book

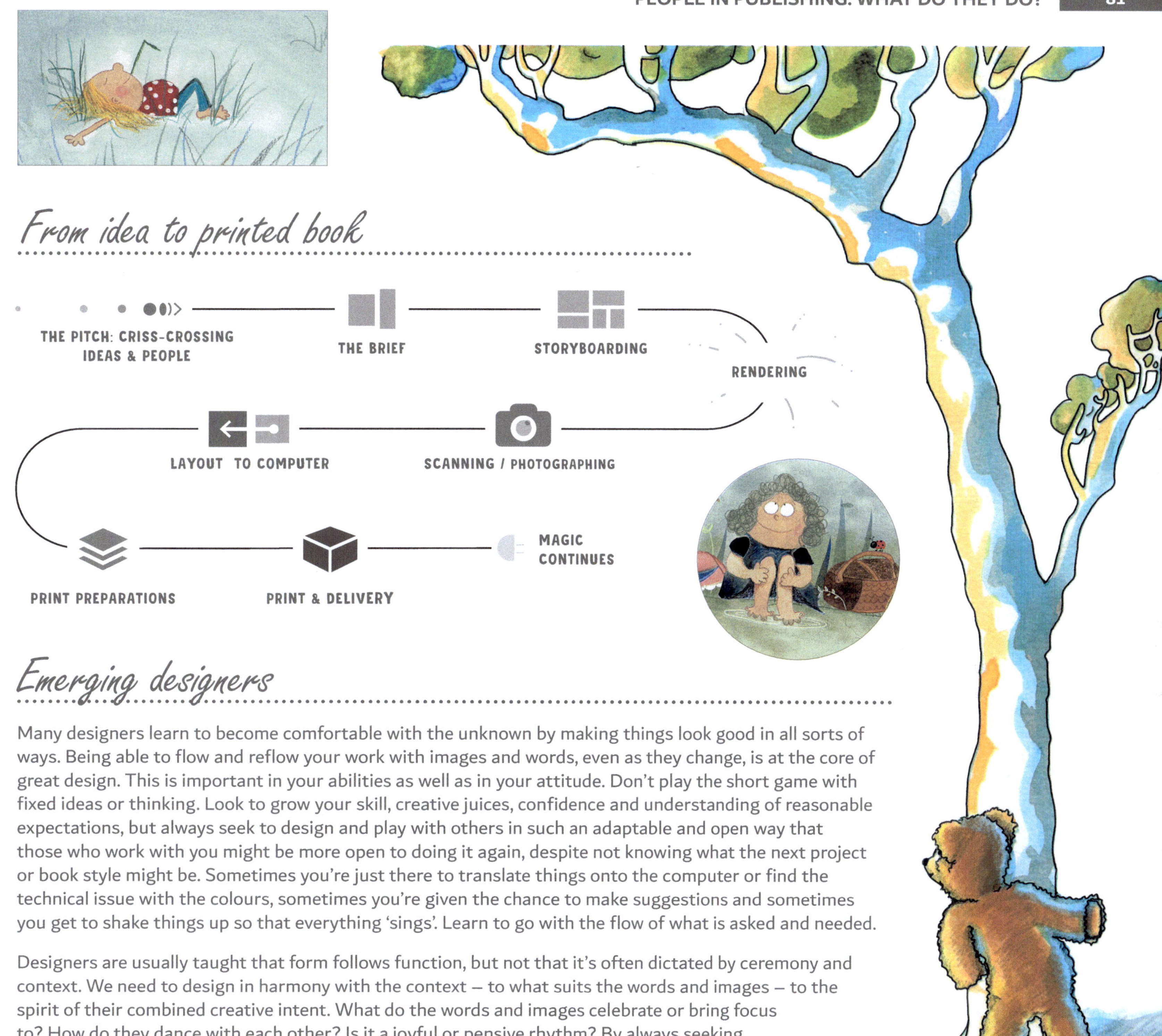

Emerging designers

Many designers learn to become comfortable with the unknown by making things look good in all sorts of ways. Being able to flow and reflow your work with images and words, even as they change, is at the core of great design. This is important in your abilities as well as in your attitude. Don't play the short game with fixed ideas or thinking. Look to grow your skill, creative juices, confidence and understanding of reasonable expectations, but always seek to design and play with others in such an adaptable and open way that those who work with you might be more open to doing it again, despite not knowing what the next project or book style might be. Sometimes you're just there to translate things onto the computer or find the technical issue with the colours, sometimes you're given the chance to make suggestions and sometimes you get to shake things up so that everything 'sings'. Learn to go with the flow of what is asked and needed.

Designers are usually taught that form follows function, but not that it's often dictated by ceremony and context. We need to design in harmony with the context – to what suits the words and images – to the spirit of their combined creative intent. What do the words and images celebrate or bring focus to? How do they dance with each other? Is it a joyful or pensive rhythm? By always seeking to understand the ceremony, culture and tensions of the work you are handling, the layout design can play with and hold the balance, as needed. **— Rae Ainsworth, designer**

PRINTER

IN THE CHILDREN'S BOOK SECTOR, ALMOST ALL BOOK SALES ARE IN PRINT, AND EBOOKS ARE A VERY DISTANT SECOND. IT MEANS THAT PRINTERS ARE A VERY IMPORTANT PART OF THE PROCESS (AS, INDEED, THEY ARE IN ADULT PUBLISHING).

Publishers may use printers in Australia, which is the case for most paperback books, or overseas printers, which is usually the case with hardcovers, such as picture books. There are several specialised book printers in Australia, along with those who print books as well as other media. In terms of overseas printers, China and Singapore are the countries most used by Australian publishers.

We are all familiar with the concept of printing. But how do printers work with publishers?

Printing has to be timed so the stock of the book is available to distributors two or three months before the book is published, and often more than that (especially if dealing with overseas printers with much longer delivery times). Publishers will contact their account manager at the selected printer according to a well-planned schedule and provide the printer with the specs for the book.

Fil always suspected that her cat Harry could talk if he really tried. Sometimes she even dreamed about it. But it was still a shock when he did start talking, on the worst afternoon of her life—or one of them. She seemed to be having a lot of them lately...
And Harry was the only one in the family who knew the way out of the tangle.

A fresh, lively junior novel by Jenny Blackford, winner of the 2020 Davitt Award for Best Children's Crime Novel, with fabulous illustrations by Kristin Devine, winner of the 2019 New England Illustration prize.

ISBN 978-0-64881-540-2

9 780648 815402 >

Fil and Harry

JENNY BLACKFORD

Fil AND Harry

JENNY BLACKFORD

These will include:

- trim size (size of the book)
- stock (type of paper used for the internal pages and cover)
- ink and embellishments (cover decisions such as matte, gloss and foils, and whether internal pages have coloured or black and white illustrations)
- binding
- quantity of copies and where they should be delivered (e.g. to the publisher's distributor and the publisher for marketing).

From these specs, printers will put together a quote that includes 'prepress' information. The latter can involve the kind of proof copies they will provide to the publisher, such as 'hard proofs' and 'ozalids', which are usually for picture books, or digital 'soft proofs', which are usually for novels and chapter books. The proofs will vary in their ability to accurately represent the final look and feel of a finished book. Some proofs are for positional accuracy only. Some, such as Indigo proofs, aim to provide a realistic representation of the final copy by using a sample of the actual paper with the specified inks.

Once everything has been decided, a date for sending the book file to the printer is set. When the final file has been created, it is called 'print-ready'. The print-ready file will go directly to the printer through a file transfer service (most printers have their own), and they will create a proof to be sent to the publisher. This proof will be checked by the publisher's team, and any errors or glitches will be picked up. Once the proof has been checked and approved by the publisher, then the printing job starts. When all the stock has been printed, it is sent to the delivery address or addresses that the publisher has specified. Then the work of distribution will begin.

DISTRIBUTOR

THE PEOPLE WHO ENSURE BOOKS GET TO BOOKSHOPS AND LIBRARIES ARE CALLED DISTRIBUTORS. WITHOUT THEM, NO BOOK WOULD GET TO ITS INTENDED READERSHIP.

Mikhail Strogoff spurred his horse on across a peaty plain...

Distribution may be handled in-house, co-operatively between publishing houses or with independent operators. Yet, despite the importance of distributors, many authors aren't clear on what is involved in the business of distribution, and most people outside the industry don't even know it exists.

So, what do distributors do? They work with publisher clients to get stock of their books into sales outlets. Books are sent directly from the printer to the distributor's warehouse, and orders from bookshops and libraries will be filled from there. If the publisher has their own sales reps, then the reps will show the publisher's catalogues to bookshops, and all the distributor has to do is fill the orders. However, for small publishers without the means to have their own sales reps, their distributors will act in both roles.

This is the case for independent distributors such as Peribo, NewSouth Books, Woodslane, Exisle Publishing and Novella Distribution. Each month, the distributor's reps, working from multi-publisher monthly catalogues that the distributor creates, will discuss each title with their bookseller clients. Orders will then be taken, and once the stock of books arrives from the printer, those orders can be filled. Distributors work on titles several months in advance (the actual period depends on the distributor) so it is the publisher's responsibility to make sure all information about the book, plus cover images and samples, are provided in the required time frame. Most distributors deal with a wide range of books; a few specialise in certain types of books. Self-published authors and publishers may also choose to go to a distributor.

Distributors charge publishers a percentage of the recommended retail price (RRP) for their services. Depending on whether the publisher owns the distributor or the distributor is independent of the publisher, the percentage varies, but it can go up to around 70 per cent. This may seem very high, but distributors must give discounts within that to bookshops, libraries and other outlets, as well as pay for infrastructure (such as warehouses), staff and transport of books.

Especially for small publishers, trying to distribute books themselves soon leads to the realisation that it is very complex, time-consuming and expensive. Online direct orders via a publisher's website can work, to some extent, with individual buyers, but it is often only an adjunct to traditional distribution, which reaches far more outlets in much less time. Bookshops also generally prefer to interact with distributors, not directly with publishers.

RIGHTS MANAGERS

RIGHTS MANAGERS WORK FOR PUBLISHERS TO SELL SUBSIDIARY RIGHTS TO BOOKS.

These mainly centre on international rights for distribution outside Australia and New Zealand by an overseas publisher, which may include other English-language territories, like the USA, UK and Canada, or in translation.

A publisher's rights manager will go to international book fairs to present books to overseas publishers, and they will approach publishers directly throughout the year, online or in person. It's a very busy role as selling rights involves both new books and titles on the 'backlist', such as those published in previous years. A rights manager's work may also include selling audiobook rights to a specialist audio publisher, such as Bolinda or Wavesound, and selling rights to film, radio, TV, and extracts or serial publications.

In big and medium publishers, the rights manager is in-house and may have other staff dealing with audio, film or TV rights. This happens in some smaller publishers too, but many small publishers instead use the services of an independent international rights management agency, which has a contract to sell international rights on behalf of the publisher. One such international rights manager is the ALC Agency https://alcagency.com/, which represents small Australian publishers such as Christmas Press, Dirt Lane Press, Wombat Books, New Frontier Publishing, Red Paper Kite and more. Just as in-house rights managers work with sub-agents based in different countries, an independent rights manager such as ALC works with numerous agents in different territories to represent a publisher and their list. Occasionally, rights management may also be part of a distribution deal, for example, Little Pink Dog Books titles are represented by Exisle Publishing, which distributes in Australia, New Zealand, the UK and the US but also manages the sale of international rights in translation territories.

SALES REPS

SALES REPS (SHORT FOR REPRESENTATIVES) WORK DIRECTLY WITHIN A PUBLISHING HOUSE – THIS IS THE CASE FOR ALL BIG AND MEDIUM PUBLISHERS – OR ARE BASED WITHIN THE PUBLISHER'S DISTRIBUTOR. ALL SALES REPS, REGARDLESS OF LOCATION, DO SIMILAR WORK.

Months before a book's release, they contact booksellers, libraries and other outlets with catalogues of new and backlisted books. Using these, they work to persuade buyers to order copies for their store or library. To sell effectively, reps need to have a good sense of the books they are promoting, so there's a lot of work beforehand to familiarise themselves with the publisher's list. At the beginning of each year, there will usually be an in-house sales conference for reps to become familiar with the books. If it's within a publishing house, editors and publishers will talk to the reps, present the new books on their list and highlight key selling features of the titles while reps ask questions and make comments. When the reps are based within a distributor, they will be representing the books of several publishers, so the sales conference will feature many presentations.

In this instance, the conference will usually follow the same pattern as an in-house sales conference. Sometimes writers and illustrators will also be invited to make a virtual or in-person presentation. If, as a writer or illustrator, you are invited to go to one, don't miss out. It's a great opportunity to talk directly to the people who have the task of enthusing booksellers and librarians about your book – and if you can enthuse the reps, your publisher will be very happy.

MARKETING AND PUBLICITY

MARKETING AND PUBLICITY ARE IMPORTANT PARTS OF ENSURING A BOOK NOT ONLY GETS TO READERS BUT ALSO REACHES THE *RIGHT* READERS.

Specialised marketing and publicity staff are employed in many big, medium and small publishers, but freelance or contract staff may also be used on occasion. In some small publishers with very few employees, core team members could do the marketing and publicity from other fields.

Wearing many hats is a common feature of small press publishing!

Whether in-house or freelance, marketing and promotion staff will work on campaigns for the book months ahead of publication. After reading the book (or being briefed thoroughly on it), they prepare a marketing and publicity plan, which will include:

- possible involvement in areas such as covers and blurbs
- deciding on the 'hook' or the element of the book that might catch the most attention. This is done in consultation with the author (and illustrator, if it's a picture book)
- sending out questionnaires for authors and illustrators about themselves and the book, usually to get background information and a few useful quotes
- liaising with designers about catalogues and other marketing materials
- supporting sales reps by creating advance information kits about the book and creators
- sending out press releases and advance information about the book and its creators to review outlets, whether print, online, broadcast or podcast. If interest is expressed, sending books out as print copies or final PDF files; interviews with the creators may also be organised
- arranging for the creation of promotional 'extras', such as bookmarks and flyers
- organising book tours, launches and author events (whether in person or online)
- pitching the book and its creators to literary festivals.

Much of the work by marketers and publicists is done through phone calls, emails and online meetings but can also involve face-to-face meetings with influential people in publishing, media or otherwise. Publicists may also be assigned to work with just a few books or authors, which is particularly the case with big-name authors.

In the past, the marketing and publicity staff took care of most of the advertising required to spread the word about a book, and the author just had to turn up to talk about their work. These days, however, authors are expected to do more to help with publicity and marketing efforts, especially through social media. Today, virtual or in-person launches may also be organised by authors rather than publishers. In the section on 'Getting published', you will find some useful advice from book marketing experts on how authors can best help their publisher in the promotion of their books.

A HOUSE OF MUD
A HOUSE OF MUD
Sophie Masson
Katrina Fisher

I'M A dirty DINOSAUR

Selkie Stories

ONCE UPON A CHRISTMAS

KENSY AND MAX
THRILLS, SPILLS, ADVENTURE AND MYSTERY!
KENSY MAX

ACQUIRING A MANUSCRIPT

AT THE HEART OF PUBLISHING IS THE ACQUISITION PROCESS. THIS IS HOW PUBLISHERS ACQUIRE AUTHORS' AND AUTHORSTRATORS' BOOKS FOR PUBLICATION.

An author's unpublished manuscript (MS) may be acquired through:

- a formal submissions process online or by post
- a direct approach by the author to a publisher
- a pitch event run by such organisations as the Australian Society of Authors and the New England Writers' Centre
- a direct approach by an author's agent
- the publisher directly commissioning the author. This can include a multi-author series created by a publisher, such as Scholastic's *Australia's Great War* series, Penguin's *Our Australian Girl* series or Wild Dingo Press's *Aussie STEM Star* series.

In large and medium publishing houses, acquisitions meetings are where proposals or submissions are discussed and formally held every month or two; in small publishing houses, these will happen less often and more informally after a submissions period. For the acquisitions meeting, commissioning editors or other senior editors build a case for a book to be published, showing the MS to other members of the team.

THE ACQUISITIONS PROCESS

A commissioning document may be produced that sets out a description of the book, the pros and cons of taking it on, the author's profile and more. For picture book manuscripts, a proposed illustrator may also have been sought, and samples by them will form part of the case for the book. Illustrators can be people the publisher has worked with before, those proposed by an agent and those discovered through a submissions process or online sources, such as Style File and Instagram.
For chapter books, junior fiction and middle-grade fiction, illustrators are usually decided on after the author has been contracted.

At this stage, a document setting out an initial business case may also be compiled, which will include aspects like cost of production, what age range the book is aimed at, what markets will be targeted and how many copies will be printed.

At an acquisitions meeting, each proposal will be presented by the editor championing it and discussed with the whole team, including finance, sales, design, marketing and rights. In small presses, of course, a team member may wear several different hats. Initial decisions may be made at the meeting, or editors may be asked to provide more information for a later meeting. If the proposal is received favourably, a draft publishing contract will be drawn up and sent to the author or author's agent. This will set out details such as the timing of publication, delivery of final MS, advance to be paid, royalties, and subsidiary rights, such as overseas editions, film rights and more (see our glossary of contract terms in 'Your part in the publication process' on page 100).

If the contract is accepted and signed by the author, then book production moves to the next stage. For a picture book, the selected illustrator will also be contracted at the same time. For an illustrated book, the illustrator may be decided on and contracted a little later.

He had taken the telegram and read it...

COMMISSIONING AND BRIEFING THE ILLUSTRATOR

ON THE PREVIOUS PAGE, IT WAS NOTED THAT THE ILLUSTRATOR MAY ALREADY BE PART OF THE 'PACKAGE' PRESENTED AT THE ACQUISITIONS MEETING (IN THE CASE OF PICTURE BOOKS AND ILLUSTRATED STORYBOOKS).

They may also come on board after the author has been contracted (in the case of other illustrated works, such as chapter books, junior fiction, poetry and plays). For some kinds of non-fiction, where photographs are used, a photographer will also be commissioned.

Illustrators, like authors, work with publishers under a contract. As well as the standard clauses, the contract will specify details, such as the number and type of illustrations required (e.g. colour or black and white), when and how illustrations should be delivered, and payment (e.g. advance and royalty or outright fee). Once the contracts have been accepted and signed by both parties, the next stage begins. In the case of picture books and storybooks, the illustrator will already have read the author's text and agreed to create the visual world.

The publisher or commissioning editor who is overseeing the project will then get in touch to discuss aspects like storyboards, roughs and samples (for more details, see 'Picture books' on page 32). In other instances, the illustrator will be briefed by the publisher about what is needed.

For chapter books and junior fiction, requirements include black and white internal illustrations and a coloured cover illustration. The illustrator will be sent the whole MS to read, and the discussion will then centre around what scenes in the book might be illustrated.

For longer books, such as middle-grade fiction, where only a cover illustration may be required, the illustrator will be sent a package of briefing information, such as a complete outline of the story and important characters. The decisions will then focus on possible themes for the cover illustration.

And so it was that Mikhail Strogoff was brought before the Tsar...

Sometimes, however, an illustrator may also request the full MS to be fully aware of what the story entails. Similarly, with a non-fiction book, an illustrator or photographer may be briefed on specific aspects by the publisher or be sent the whole MS.

In all cases, the illustrator works closely with the publishing team throughout several stages of the book, such as character design, storyboard creation and different drafts, which end with the final artworks. The author will also be involved but usually only at certain points of the process.

WORKING ON PRODUCTION

AT THIS STAGE, THE ILLUSTRATOR AND AUTHOR HAVE BEEN CONTRACTED AND BRIEFED, AND WORK HAS STARTED IN EARNEST ON PRODUCTION OF THE BOOK.

EDITING

THE EDITOR WORKS CLOSELY WITH BOTH THE AUTHOR AND THE PUBLISHER TO ENSURE THAT THE TEXT IS IN THE BEST SHAPE IT CAN POSSIBLY BE.

As described in the page about editors in people in publishing, this process goes through several stages. The editor works from the digital document supplied by the author and agreed to by the publisher, reads the text carefully (whether for a picture book or a longer work), then proceeds to edit on-screen. Everything from simple formatting changes (such as font types or line spacing), minor errors (such as typos) and more complex content issues (such as plot, character, tone and pace) will be examined. Attention to spelling and grammar errors will, of course, also form part of this. Using track changes and the comments function on the document, the editor suggests changes and solutions to the author. Several edits will be done, with the first edit being the most comprehensive. Each time, the author is sent the edited document to review, revise and make their own changes. This process usually takes several months to complete.

ARTWORK AND LAYOUT

FOR PICTURE BOOKS, THE ARTWORK AND LAYOUT PROCESS IS LIKE THE EDITING PROCESS FOR LONGER WRITTEN WORKS. THERE ARE SEVERAL STAGES, FROM ROUGHS AND STORYBOARDS TO FINISHED IMAGES AND LAYOUT.

The illustrator works closely with the publishing team throughout several drafts. An early draft may be created on paper, which is then scanned and made into a file for sharing and editing, but later drafts are generally made directly on-screen. In publishing houses with an art director, that person may oversee the creation of the book's visual world.

In others, the commissioning editor may do so, while in yet others, especially in small press, it is the publisher. In all publishing houses, the design team will also be closely involved. These processes may also happen for longer written works where illustration occurs, but the process will not be as lengthy or detailed.

DESIGN

THE DESIGNER, WHETHER IN-HOUSE OR FREELANCE, WILL BE WORKING WITH THE PUBLISHER AND ILLUSTRATOR, AND THEIR WORK IS CENTRAL TO THE GENERAL LOOK OF THE BOOK.

The designer will be briefed by the publisher on technical aspects, such as format (hardcover or paperback), the book's dimensions (known as trim size), paper stock (the type of paper used for the cover and internals), whether the book is full colour throughout and any special effects (such as foil on a book title). The designer needs to know these details so that their design fits the book's physical aspects exactly. For picture books, design is an important of the process, and designers are often involved in layout, font choice, placement of images and text, and creation of endpapers.

For longer illustrated texts, design is also an important part of the book's creation. But even in a book without internal illustrations, pages need to be designed with an awareness of fonts and formats, and the cover has to be created. Sometimes the designer will work with a commissioned illustrator on the cover of a book, but they may also be briefed to create the cover themselves.

BOOK DETAILS AND ADMINISTRATION

MEANWHILE, BOOK ADMINISTRATION DETAILS WILL ALSO NEED TO BE COMPLETED. AN ISBN, A UNIQUE IDENTIFYING NUMBER FOR EACH BOOK, WILL BE ASSIGNED, AND A BAR CODE WILL ALSO BE OBTAINED, WHICH IS NECESSARY FOR BOOKSHOP SALES.

Metadata (comprehensive book details) will need to be compiled and registered with organisations such as Thorpe-Bowker (the ISBN agency in Australia) and TitlePage (a comprehensive book data service for publishers and booksellers).

The book will also need to be registered with the National Library of Australia's Prepublication Data Service to ensure its basic details will be in the public record. An imprint page for the book, which contains copyright details and an ISBN, will be created.

An acknowledgements page will also be made, if required. A back cover blurb for the book will need to be written in consultation with the author (and illustrator, if it's a picture book).

FILE PREPARATION AND PROOFING

THE PRINT-READY FILE HAS TO BE PREPARED WELL AHEAD OF SENDING IT TO THE PRINTER.

Once editing, illustration and design have all been completed, and data has been registered, all components of the book are assembled in the InDesign program (usually by the design team) to create the file.

It is then exported as a low-resolution PDF and sent for checking and proofing to the author, illustrator, editor, designer, publisher and any proofreaders. There will be checks for errors in the text, in illustration placement (for example, if a double-spread illustration has important details cut off in the 'gutter' or the fold) and in details on the imprint page or blurb. With picture books, a paper proof file may also be created at this stage, as it is easier to spot design errors on paper. Once any corrections are incorporated by the publisher, a new file will be created and sent for another round of checking and proofing. When all parties are satisfied that everything is prepared, a print-ready file in a high-resolution PDF will be created to send to the printer.

> It is important to recognise the endless potential for editing artwork on the computer. But when the authenticity of the book is the priority, then any adjustments should be quite unnoticeable. It's reasonable to expect that artwork on internal pages should only need minor editing and colour adjustment. Anything more may indicate challenges with communication, style, scanning, artwork size or the spacing allowed for words and bleed.
> **— Rae Ainsworth, designer**

PRINTING

AS DESCRIBED IN THE 'PEOPLE IN PUBLISHING' SECTION, WELL BEFORE THE FILE IS SENT TO THE PRINTER, THE PUBLISHER WILL HAVE BRIEFED THE PRINTER ABOUT WHAT IS REQUIRED FOR THE BOOK IN TERMS OF TRIM SIZE, QUANTITY, DELIVERY, PAPER STOCK AND SO ON.

Once the file has been received by the printer, they will produce a 'soft copy' or digital proof file for further checking by the publishing team. It is very important to get these final checks absolutely right, as mistakes can be expensive! For longer written works, a soft copy proof is all that's required, but for picture books, it's important to have paper proofs as well. These will be produced by the printer, sent to the publisher and checked for colour reproduction, alignment of images, text font and more. Once the publisher is satisfied with the quality of proofs, the approval to print will be granted, but in the case of picture books, a final digital proof and a sample copy of the finished product may be required first. Advance reading copies might also be produced for the publisher's or distributor's sales reps. These will be given to key retail or library clients.

DISTRIBUTION

WHILE WORK IS PROCEEDING ON PRODUCTION OF THE BOOK, THE PUBLISHER WILL HAVE CONTACTED THE DISTRIBUTOR (FOR AN EXPLANATION OF WHAT DISTRIBUTORS DO, SEE 'DISTRIBUTOR' ON PAGE 83).

Months ahead of publication, the publisher's distributor will have been sent full information about the book so that their reps can begin selling to their bookseller and library clients. Advance reading copies may also be supplied to the distributor. As soon as the finished book is printed, an agreed amount of the stock will be sent to the distributor's warehouse so that they can promptly fulfil all orders.

OTHER PRODUCTION FORMATS

CHILDREN'S BOOK PUBLISHING IS DOMINATED BY PRINT. THIS IS BECAUSE CHILDREN AND FAMILIES GREATLY FAVOUR PRINT WHEN IT COMES TO READING BOOKS.

However, there are other publishing formats possible, such as ebooks and audiobooks. These are usually an addition to the print edition, rather than a substitute. Both ebook and audio rights are usually a part of publishing contracts, often in the 'subsidiary rights' clause.

Ebook editions are most common within those areas of children's publishing that aim at a readership of seven and over, with middle-grade novels dominating. Audiobook editions cover a wider age range, from the very young onwards. In children's publishing, audiobooks tend to be more popular than ebooks and have become even more so in recent years. The rise in digital audiobooks makes it very easy to buy, download and listen to audiobooks anywhere on any device.

Ebook editions are often created in-house by the publisher at the same time as a print edition is being prepared. Audiobooks are generally created by external audiobook production companies who employ freelance narrators, audio engineers and soundscape artists. These companies are contracted directly by the publisher to produce the book.

Alternatively, the publisher may sell audio rights to specialist audio publishers who employ an in-house production team and also distribute and market the book.

WORKING ON SALES AND PROMOTION

WHILE PRODUCTION WORK IS HAPPENING, THE PUBLICITY, SALES AND MARKETING TEAMS ARE BUSY TOO. AS WELL AS WHAT IS ALREADY DESCRIBED IN PEOPLE AND PUBLISHING, OTHER ASPECTS OF THIS WORK MAY INCLUDE:

SALES

- Preparing information for distributors
- Reaching out to bookseller and library clients, updating them on new titles and forthcoming titles, and supplying them with advance reading copies (ARCs) in hard copy or PDF
- Preparing a pre-order page on the publisher's website
- Approaching specialised schools' distributors, such as Australian Standing Orders, Lamont Books and Scholastic Book Clubs, with advance information on upcoming titles.

This is so that as many pre-sales as possible can be achieved, which will bring costs of production down and help position the book well even before official release. It will also determine the size of the print run. This work needs to be done many months ahead of publication. Well ahead of publication, too, rights managers will gather together material to present the book to international publishers at trade fairs such as Bologna, Frankfurt, London and Beijing.

PROMOTION AND PUBLICITY

- Approaching a well-known author or illustrator for a 'puff' or cover quote. If they agree, then a clean, edited PDF file of the book is sent to them to read
- Creating publicity material, such as social media hashtags and tiles, to support the author and/ or illustrator in their publicity efforts
- Supplying ARCs to selected key reviewers
- Updating information on publisher website and social media
- Liaising with the author/illustrator about availability for events, such as festivals, conferences, school visits and launches (whether in person or online)
- Liaising with the author/illustrator using any media or review contacts that they might have, and reaching out to these contacts to arrange interviews and reviews
- Preparing giveaways and other competitions
- Approaching specialist publications (such as *Magpies* Magazine, *Books+Publishing* and *Good Reading*) to enquire about editorial and advertising space
- Entering book awards such as Speech Pathology Australia Book of the Year Awards, CBCA, Premier's Literary Awards, etc.

The work of promotion and sales continues well after publication and the book's appearance on bookshop shelves. Beyond the launch of the book and initial flurry of sales and publicity, the publishing team will be working on submitting books for awards, following up on interest from overseas publishers, publicising author and illustrator appearances at events – and much more. And of course, there's always the next book on the publisher's list to be worked on!

WORKING WITH THE CHILDREN'S BOOK COMMUNITY

CHILDREN'S BOOK PUBLISHERS HAVE STRONG TIES TO THE CHILDREN'S BOOK COMMUNITY. THIS CAN INVOLVE AUTHOR/ILLUSTRATOR GROUPS, BOOKSELLERS, LIBRARIANS, READERS, SCHOOLS AND ORGANISATIONS.

Useful organisations include the Children's Book Council of Australia, the Society of Children's Book Writers and Illustrators, the Indigenous Literacy Foundation and Australia Reads (see our full list of organisations at the end of this section). These groups are very much at the heart of the publishing process, and the publishing team works on many different aspects of community engagement throughout the year.

Ways in which publishers support the children's books community include:

- facilitating author and illustrator visits in schools and libraries
- supporting author and illustrator events in bookshops
- sponsoring prizes and opportunities for authors and illustrators
- running competitions for young readers
- supplying books for charity events
- subscribing to organisations
- providing professional expertise for mentorships and judging panels
- supporting capacity-building workshops for emerging authors, illustrators, editors and designers.

CULTURAL PROTOCOLS AND SENSITIVITY

Both publishers and creators need to be mindful of the cultural protocols of Aboriginal and Torres Strait Islander peoples. Writers and illustrators planning to create work based on cultural material (for instance, traditional stories or life stories) should seek advice and permissions from the community where the stories originated. This applies to both fiction and non-fiction. A great guide on how best to do this is the digital publication *More Than Words*, by Terri Janke, Anika Valenti and Laura Curtis, available from the Australian Society of Authors https://www.asauthors.org/products/asa-resources-and-guides/more-than-words.

Also, it is important to be aware of sensitive issues when creating work based on the experiences or stories of people from any cultural community or vulnerable group other than your own. Some authors and publishers use specialised editors known as 'sensitivity readers'* to advise them, but that is not essential. What is essential, however, is to show respect and care.

(*Sensitivity readers review unpublished manuscripts to spot cultural inaccuracies, representation issues, bias, stereotypes or problematic language.)

Our contracts are quite specific and very long – currently sitting at 21 pages. They are an in-depth code of conduct in regard to the selling and licensing of Aboriginal and Torres Strait Islander titles. Magabala Books needs to be quite specific with its expectations about the cultural capital of individuals and communities, as its genesis was a result of the lack of recognition of cultural rights, community and creator stories and the pilfering of collective intellectual property rights.
— Rachel Bin Salleh, publisher, Magabala Books

BOOK SALES: HOW DOES IT WORK?

NOW THE BOOK HAS APPEARED. IT'S IN BOOKSHOPS, OTHER RETAIL OUTLETS AND LIBRARIES, AND ITS SALES RECORD BEGINS. HOW DOES IT ALL WORK?

Readers are sometimes surprised to learn that authors and illustrators are paid a small percentage of the retail price, not the full amount. Sometimes authors and illustrators are also surprised to learn that the publisher doesn't receive the sums they might imagine. As noted in the page about the distributor in people in publishing, the distributor gets a high discount – and also has to offer discounts to bookshops and libraries, which brings that percentage down for distributors as well. Other retail outlets, such as Kmart, Big W and Target, also require a high discount from publishers, and so do specialised schools distributors, such as Australian Standing Orders and Lamont Books.

This impacts the percentage paid to authors, and most contracts specify lower royalty rates for high-discount sales. (For more information on contracts, see 'Your part in the publication process' on page 100.) Selling directly on a publisher's website (especially for pre-orders) or at events (where the publisher supplies the books) may mean a bigger percentage for both publisher and author, but it is time-consuming and cannot be counted on to sell many books. And, of course, most publishers prefer to work with bookshops, libraries and distributors, who are such an important part of the industry.

Sales arrangements in the book trade operate either on a 'firm sale' basis or on 'sale and return'. Firm sale means that books are bought outright by the retailer (common in high-discount stores) or by the school distributors mentioned above. This means that although the discount is high, publishers are guaranteed the sale amount as these books cannot be returned. Library suppliers also buy on firm sale. However, most books are ordered by bookshops on 'sale or return', which means that if books aren't sold within a certain time frame, the book can be simply returned to the distributor or publisher without incurring a cost. On sales reports, this means that there will be negatives (returned books) as well as positives (sold books).

Sales reports are compiled every month by the distributor. These will show total sales for each title, plus returns, and are for in-house consumption by the publisher. The Nielsen BookScan service also provides point-of-sale data for particular titles across a wide range of publishers in Australia. These figures don't give a complete picture of a book's sales (they don't involve Australian Standing Orders and similar schools-oriented sales, for example) but they do provide an accurate picture of books sold in bookshops and high-discount outlets, as well as online retailers like Booktopia and Amazon. BookScan is a subscription service and is widely used throughout the industry. It can be used by booksellers when deciding whether to order a particular book and in what quantities. It can also be used by publishers deciding whether a particular author's previous sales record needs to be weighed up in discussions about acquiring their next manuscript, and it can be used by agents to keep track of their clients' sales. Not everyone uses BookScan – small publishers may not subscribe, for instance – but its impact on the industry is undeniable.

Finally, a note on how library sales affect author and publisher payments. Although a library book is borrowed by the reader, not sold to them, the Lending Rights system means that books will still earn payments for both creators and publishers. Some titles that may not appear to have big sales in BookScan may earn considerable Lending Rights payments. The fact that, especially with children's books, these payments may continue many years after they have first been published (as long as they stay in libraries) means another important source of income for both creators and publishers.

WHEN THINGS GO WRONG

PUBLISHING A BOOK IS A COMPLEX BUSINESS WITH MANY MOVING PARTS. MOSTLY, IT WORKS REALLY WELL.

But occasionally things go wrong – publishers are only human, after all! Here are some real-life examples of production and promotion bloopers (no names used to avoid red faces!).

- Internal pages of a book were printed upside down or in the wrong order (printer's error).
- The name of a character was changed halfway through a story and wasn't picked up in proofing. Fortunately, it was not an important character, but it was embarrassing.
- Typo in a picture book was not picked up in proofing. It was a small error, so it was able to pass.
- The wrong title on a book spine wasn't noticed in proofing. It was an expensive mistake! The book could not be sold like that at all, so the entire print run had to be discarded and a new print run ordered with the right title on the spine.
- Illustration inserts were put in the wrong place during half a print run (printer's error).
- A cover illustration slightly shifted in the printer's proof and wasn't noticed by the author, illustrator, publisher or prepress team at the printers. The print run did not need to be discarded, as it was only a small mistake. The vast majority of readers, including reviewers, did not notice either.
- Incorrect data was sent to the distributor and National Library service. It was fixed with some difficulty!
- Trim size was mixed up with another book, so it was printed in the wrong format. The printer discarded those copies and a new print run of the book was ordered.
- Stock got lost in transit (the printer was overseas, cartons of books were sent by ship, the container was mislaid and stock never arrived).
- Books for a launch didn't arrive in time at the participating bookshop.
- Books for an award were sent in after the closing date for entries.

Dealing with production bloopers is not easy and is often costly, but it is very important that respect for the author's work and a professional approach to admitting and correcting mistakes should be at the centre of how publishers deal with issues if they arise.

PITCHING TO PUBLISHERS

THE FIRST STEP IN THE SUBMISSION PROCESS IS PITCHING TO PUBLISHERS.

This may take the form of a formal pitching session direct to a publishing professional, whether in person or online; an online submission through a publisher's website; an email to a publisher; or an informal pitch at a literary event.

This must be handled subtly and carefully – do not 'bail up' a publisher or editor. Pitching can be a nerve-racking experience for a new writer or illustrator (and even for more experienced ones), and the key to a good experience is to prepare.

GENERAL TIPS FOR PREPARING TO PITCH:

- Research the publisher before making your pitch.
- Get your biography (or bio, as it is usually termed in publishing) in good shape. It should not be too long; try for no more than 75 to 100 words.
- Trim your synopsis or outline. Start with one page, and then go to half a page, then a paragraph, then a single sentence. Each type will help you drill down to the heart of your proposal.
- Prepare your oral pitch by practising your delivery and timing – rehearse, rehearse, rehearse. A one-page handout can be used as a memory aid during the pitch and be given to the publisher afterwards if they are interested.
- Craft a good query or cover letter if preparing to pitch online or by email. Like a blurb, the point is to entice and to make the reader want to ask for more.
- Get your material – your manuscript, for writers, and your portfolio, for illustrators – in good shape. Seek advice from the professionals.
- Create a representative portfolio of illustrations, not just a sample of proposed work. Make it clear if you are interested in illustrating other people's work, whether picture books or book covers.

Advice about preparation

On bios and author profiles:

A bio is not the same as a CV, although there are similarities. The big difference is in structure and format. CVs are set out as formal lists with subheadings and dates. Bios are more like mini-stories. They should give a flavour of the person behind them without being too familiar. Consider how your bio is going to establish your profile now and in the future. Relevant information, including a publication record, is important.

If possible, utilise a digital platform, whether that be a website, blog or social media engagement, and include any digital links at the end of your bio (or your query letter). Incidentally, it is not essential for an author to engage in social media, although it is useful; but an author website is, to my mind, essential. Publishers who might be interested in your work will want to investigate online, and a well-presented website with good information is the easiest entry point. This is the case for both writers and illustrators, although a great Instagram page with a decent following can function in the same way for an illustrator.
— Sophie Masson, author and publisher

Presentation of manuscripts:

First impressions are important. Nothing impresses more than manuscript presentation. Storytelling and quality writing must always take first place, but if the manuscript is littered with typographical errors and inconsistencies, it sends a clear message. It tells me the author is not professional and does not take pride in his or her work. So always format your manuscript to the publisher's specifications, if they have them, or follow standard professional specifications.
— Dmetri Kakmi, author and former editor at Penguin Books

Self-editing:

First impressions are important. Nothing impresses more than manuscript presentation. One of the biggest mistakes a writer can make when examining their manuscript is to remain a writer. This may sound nonsensical, but the best piece of advice for self-editing is to become a reader. Pretend your manuscript is one that you plucked from a shelf and jot down any errors (briefly) in the margins as you read the whole way through. Once the issues have been addressed, repeat the process until you can enjoy the work wholeheartedly as a reader.
— Sharnee Rawson, editor

Outline/Synopsis:

Is your synopsis as snappy as your manuscript? It has to be! That's the first thing I read. If you can't write an interesting synopsis, then how do I know you can write an entire book? **— Beattie Alvarez, commissioning editor, Christmas Press**

Advice from publishers and agents

Check the publisher's guidelines before submitting. It saves both you and the publisher time, effort and money. And keep your pitch letter to a minimum. No publisher wants to hear about how your friends, family and kids think your manuscript is fantastic. It's up to the publisher to decide that. No publisher likes to get hassled by authors or illustrators. Be prepared to wait at least three months for a response. **— Paul Collins, director, Ford Street Publishing**

My top tip for submitting to publishers is to do your homework. Check their website first for any submission guidelines – these may be buried in an obscure corner of the website, but nearly all publishers have them. Pay attention to what the guidelines say. If they're not taking submissions, then don't submit to them; if they are only looking for picture book texts, then don't send a young adult novel; and if they have a particular day or time to receive submissions (Allen & Unwin has Friday Pitch), then take note of those constraints. It's also useful to get a feel for their list and whether your submission might fit by checking their website or in bookstores for the types of books they publish. **— Eva Mills, publishing director, Books for Children and Young Adults, Allen & Unwin**

If you're a writer of picture books, you don't need to worry about the illustrations at the submission stage. The publisher will contract an illustrator separately and will likely have their ideas about ideal collaborators, which they'll share with you. Publishers have great visual imaginations, so unless an illustration note is essential to understanding something about the story not evident in the words alone, leave illustration descriptions off your submission. **— Chren Byng, head of Australian Children's Publishing, HarperCollins Australia**

It's a good idea to submit to more than one publisher or agent at a time (unless their guidelines say not to), but if you get an offer, contact the others – no matter how quiet they have been – before you agree to the offer. You never know when someone else is just about to say yes or wants the opportunity to finish reading, and giving them a short window to get back to you means you are not burning bridges for future submissions. **— Alexandra Adsett, principal at Alex Adsett Literary Agency**

Oral pitches:

- Speak clearly and confidently without rushing. Use notes if you want, but don't read from a script. Say a few words about yourself, your experience and your publication record (if any).
- Keep to the time you are allocated, and be clear as to what you are pitching. Do not recount the whole plot or outline of your book. If you have a great opening line, use it!
- Let publishers know if you have written a complete manuscript. However, do not bring entire manuscripts or expect publishers to read samples on the spot.
- Show that you are well-read in the genre that you are writing in by making a subtle mention that might help publishers and editors to place your work, but avoid claiming that your book is just like some bestseller. For instance, 'I've been influenced by ...' or 'I like reading XYZ'. Publishers like to know you are a reader too! Also, do not talk about 'the market' but about readers or audience.

Submission moment online:

- Follow the publisher's guidelines on submissions! This applies to both writers and illustrators. Read all the guidelines carefully and follow them exactly.
- Check the format of the initial material carefully, and only send that. For example, if the specifications are a covering letter, synopsis and three sample chapters in a Word doc with double-spaced Times New Roman 12 point, this means you do exactly that. Do not send more, and do not send the entire manuscript in, say, Curly Stars font as a PDF. The editor will not read it.
- Don't expect feedback on your proposal if you are unsuccessful. You will likely get an automatic acknowledgement that your submission has been received. Most publishers' submissions guidelines specify a time period (often 3 to 6 months) while they consider proposals. They will also state that you won't hear from them unless they are interested in your proposal, so don't send any follow-up emails unless they have requested your manuscript.
- Expect progress reports to take time, even if they have requested your manuscript. If you haven't heard anything for eight weeks or so, you could send an email politely asking if they received the manuscript (just in case!) but without sounding as though you want a quick answer. Remember, it's always easier for people to say no – give them no reason to!

Pitching to an agent:

- Let them get a sense of you and the material you are writing or want to write. Show an agent that you are someone who they could easily work with over the long term, and who is prepared to take advice. While publishers are interested in looking at an individual work, agents are principally interested in assessing you as a potential client they can represent to publishers more than once, with more than one book.
- Show different aspects of your portfolio of illustrations so an agent can assess possible placement with different publishers. Unless you are an authorstrator, a lot of illustrators' work comes from illustrating other people's texts, which involves close collaboration with publishers throughout the process. The agent needs to see if you can work collaboratively.

YOUR PART IN THE PUBLICATION PROCESS

Many creators celebrate when their pitch has been successful, and their work has been accepted for publication. What's next? In our publishing process pages, we describe the production journey of a book from the perspective of the publisher, including the work they and their team have to do. But what about you, as the writer or illustrator? What should you expect? In this section, we look at your part in the process and getting the most from prepublication.

1. THE CONTRACT

A publishing contract (sometimes called a publishing agreement) is the central legal document that writers and illustrators will encounter when their work is acquired by a publisher. On this page, you will find a brief overview of the central terms of a typical contract, but please note that these are just the basics and individual contracts will vary. For more information, we recommend the recent book *How to be an Author* (2021) by Georgina Richter and Deborah Hunn, Fremantle Press, which has an excellent chapter on contracts. Once you have a contract, and if you don't have an agent, consider approaching the Australian Society of Authors' contract advice service for the clarification of details.

Note, however, that while it's important to look at the terms of a contract and understand what you're looking at, you can't change each term or bombard your prospective publisher with tweaks. Remember that a contract implies rights and responsibilities on both sides – the publishers and the creators. Check out the practical advice and observations from agents, authors and publishers, following the overview.

QUICK OVERVIEW OF STANDARD PUBLISHING CONTRACT TERMS

Grant of licence: the rights you are licensing to the publisher for publication in Australia and New Zealand, and potentially worldwide, in all formats. Grant of licence also describes for how long you are granting subsidiary rights. The latter will be fully described in a later clause.

Copyright: guaranteeing your work remains your property and your name will feature prominently on the book.

Warranty: asks the author to warrant that the work is original to them and does not infringe anyone else's copyright.

Delivery: the release of the manuscript and illustrations. Usually includes timing on editing and other aspects of publishing.

Publication: prospective publication date and RRP.

Advance: payment to a creator when a contract is signed. The amount is estimated according to projected royalties; however, not all publishers pay an advance.

Royalties: once an advance is 'earned out', royalties are paid on a sliding scale as a percentage of RRP and net receipts (the latter is for sales to high-discount stores like Big W and Kmart). A rising scale may be included, which means if books sell more than a specified number of copies, a higher royalty will be paid. Note that while picture book illustrators share in royalties with the writer, illustrators of novels will often be paid a one-off outright fee instead of royalties. A one-off fee will apply for individual stories in anthologies.

Subsidiary rights: extra rights granted to the publisher, such as overseas editions of the work, radio, TV and film rights, serial rights and reprographic rights (where your work is legally reproduced, usually by schools and universities). This clause will specify the percentage paid to you for such sales.

Author/illustrator copies: how many free copies of your book you'll get, and what discount you are entitled to if you want to buy more copies.

Royalty accounting: statements of your sales and royalties (usually twice a year).

Termination of contract and reversion of rights: why and how a contract may be terminated by either the publisher or the creator, and how and when rights will be reverted to the creator.

Assignment: the publisher cannot 'assign' or pass on the agreement to any third party without the author's consent and vice versa. This is important in case the publisher goes out of business.

Advice from agents, authors and publishers

Trying to explain the book-publishing model (including booksellers, distributors, returns, freight, commissions, bulk orders) is very difficult and many people find it hard to get their head around this structure. Another challenge is letting the creator know that we don't keep the other 90 per cent, as opposed to their percentage of royalty. **— Rachel Bin Salleh, publisher, Magabala Books**

Don't assume you have no negotiating power just because you're a debut author. When you and your first book are an unknown, you have all the potential in the world, so ask questions and consider if it's worth accepting the first offer. Always make sure, for instance, that there is a fair reversion clause in the contract. Publishing contracts often last for a long time, and a good reversion clause ensures that if the publisher isn't maintaining a certain level of sales (e.g. 100 copies in 12 months), the author can reclaim their rights. Another contract recommendation is to watch out for the fine print in the royalties, especially the high-discount clause. Publishers can reduce the author's royalty if they offer particularly high discounts to bookstores, but this should only apply in special circumstances, not on everyday sales. Regular bookshop discounts range from 35 per cent to 55 per cent, so never agree to a high-discount clause that reduces your royalty unless the discounts offered are higher than this. **— Alexandra Adsett, principal at Alex Adsett Literary Agency**

If the publisher won't negotiate on something important to you, don't sign. Once the contract is signed, you're bound by it, no matter how unfair it might be. Authors have more options than ever before to get published, so just walk away. **— Ian Irvine, author**

We see a contract as a framework document that forms the basis for a mutually beneficial relationship. No one wants to spend too much time on new authors and illustrators who are difficult to work with from the start. Sometimes, for example, the financial expectations of authors and illustrators are a long way off from the reality of the situation, at least as far as small publishers are concerned. At times, contracts that have been checked and approved by many parties, including literary agents and the ASA, have become overly complex, with major law firm involvement. This can be a very frustrating experience. **— Peter Creamer, co-director at Little Pink Dog Books**

2. THE EXPERIENCE OF THE EDITING PROCESS

In other sections, we have looked at how editors work and the stages of the editing process. These, of course, differ according to what type of book is being edited. For instance, editing a picture book will involve editing the text, then performing further edits as the illustrator's storyboard and samples are created. Suggested edits and comments are made on both words and illustrations. A novel, meanwhile, will go through a structural edit, a copy edit (or two) and a proof edit (or two). Generally, books that feature illustrations and text (for instance, illustrated storybooks, chapter books, junior fiction and non-fiction) will need to have editing and design attention paid to the pictures and words. This will be even more important with picture books.

It's important to remember that editing is about getting your work in the best possible shape. It can be a bit of a shock opening the edited file of your text to find it full of suggestions, corrections and comments, with track changes flagged in different colours. Take a deep breath and take time to read the edit carefully to see why the editor has made those choices. Working effectively with an editor means being prepared to listen to what they say, while also being ready

to discuss any points of difference. Editorial relationships generally work well, as long as there is mutual respect.

It's common in structural edits for editors to explain all their changes in comments in the margin, while in copyediting and proof editing, special terms and abbreviations may be used. These can include sp, indicating a misspelt word; lc, meaning put in lower case; caps, meaning put in capital letters; and so on. Some editors use a style guide, which is a document that shows the consistency of formatting within the book, such as types of chapter headings, what types of quotation marks are used for direct speech (single or double), how dates and numbers are shown (i.e. in numerals or words) and how hyphenation works. The style guide may be shared with the author.

It's important to adhere to editing schedules and not to keep the editor waiting on your revisions, but it is also important to take your time. You need to absorb, reflect and then act on the editor's suggestions and recommendations.

Remember that you can still make more structural changes to your book until the copy edit is complete. After that, you should only make minor changes and go over the proof edit carefully. Once these have been completed, there will be no further possibility of catching errors. A useful suggestion is to ask a good reader you know – a friend or family member perhaps, but one who hasn't read your manuscript – to read the proof and see if they can spot any errors. Of course, the publisher will have proofreaders as well.

Advice from editors and publishers

Editing can feel like a focus on your manuscript's flaws, instead of its strengths. It can be a challenging process for creators as your emotions are involved. Effective editing is not just about the absence of errors, it's also about a detailed reading of the manuscript from the audience's point of view. Look at the errors you've made, learn from them and build from them. Your mistakes can be the basis of your best work. **— Jen Scanlan, editor**

By all means, stick to your guns if you 100 per cent disagree with an editor's suggestion. However, the editor is there to improve your manuscript. Disagree at your own peril. **— Paul Collins, director, Ford Street Publishing**

3. THE EXPERIENCE OF THE DESIGN PROCESS

We have looked at how designers work in other sections. How will you, as creator, be involved in that process?

The answer is that it will depend on what type of book you have created. If it is a picture book, and you are an authorstrator, you will have a substantial say in the book's design. If you are the author of a picture book text, you will have some say, especially for the cover, and you will be sent draft storyboards, sample pictures and design ideas to comment on, but it is the illustrator working with the publisher and designer who will be more closely involved. This is the same for illustrated storybooks.

Outside of picture books and illustrated storybooks, there is less creator input. The writer of a longer text-based work will certainly have a say in cover ideas but is unlikely to be consulted on internal page design. Illustrators who have been contracted to provide any pictures for such works will have a say in the design, especially in the placement of images, but most design decisions will reside with the publisher, and this stipulation will often be included in publishing contracts. The exception might be when a creator is both the writer and illustrator of a longer work – for example, an illustrated non-fiction book – where the creator may create a draft design that will then be developed in consultation with the publisher.

4. MARKETING AND PROMOTION: HOW YOU CAN HELP

We've seen the process of marketing and promotion in other sections, but these days, no creator can expect publishers to do all the work. So how can you help in the most effective way?

Firstly, reach out to your publisher and find out what publicity and marketing strategies they are already planning, and then think about how you could add something of value to this. For example, do you have any contacts in your local media who might be interested in a story? Do you know any book bloggers and podcasters?

Think of other ways you could help the promotion of your book. A YouTube channel is a good tool for highlighting an author and their work in a very immediate way. Populate your channel with short, simple videos you make yourself, such as a video reading of an extract and audio-enabled PowerPoint slide shows about aspects of your book or your creative process. Add some professional material, too, if you can afford it. Perhaps commission a producer to create a video trailer for your book.

Outside of video, you can create a blog or social media posts about different aspects of your book and schedule them to appear prerelease and shortly after. Some publishers are happy to do launches, others not so much as launches can use a lot of staff time and work best for the creator's circle of family and friends rather than a general audience. If your publisher isn't keen, don't despair. You can organise a launch yourself, and the publisher will certainly support that effort with promotion and the assurance that stock gets to your chosen bookstore.

When planning your launch, you need to organise it well in advance. Consider aspects such as, what size launch do you want? Where would you like it to be? What time is best? Who will 'run' the launch – yourself, the bookseller or an MC? Who will you ask to launch the book? Will there be catering, and if so, how much is your budget? How are you going to spread the word? You could choose to do an online launch rather than an in person one. If so, you need to decide whether you'd like to have a 'live' event on Zoom, Facebook or another platform, or whether you prefer to do a prerecorded launch, which can be watched at your audience's leisure. You can check out an example of a prerecorded book launch for Sophie Masson and Cheryl Orsini's chapter book *Four on the Run* at United Publishers of Armidale https://www.unitedpublishersofarmidale.net/virtual-launches.html.

Advice from marketing and publicity experts

Marketing your book starts with you and it starts well before the book is acquired by a publisher. A good children's book creator knows their market and shapes their work to suit it. Think about your audience, research them and spend time with them. Get to know the other books on the market that your audience already likes and reads – what makes them work, and what will you do to make yours sit in the same space but still stand out? Your publisher will love collaborating with you if you already have a good sense of your audience and market positioning. **— Tash Besliev, publisher, Children's Books, Affirm Press**

Get advice from industry professionals. Join organisations like the Australian Society of Authors, participate in events and conferences, follow and learn from fellow authors, illustrators, editors and designers, and develop your writing community. Make it your business to learn more about marketing and distribution, publicity and promotions, and the broader publishing industry – booksellers, libraries, associations and experienced marketing professionals. The more you know, the more you can discover opportunities for selling and promoting your book. **— Rachael McDiarmid, director, RM Marketing Services**

ALTERNATIVE PUBLISHING MODELS

MOST PUBLISHERS, WHETHER BIG OR SMALL, WORK WITH WHAT IS SOMETIMES KNOWN AS THE 'TRADITIONAL' PUBLISHING MODEL. THAT IS, THE PUBLISHER BEARS ALL THE COSTS OF PRODUCING, DISTRIBUTING AND PROMOTING, AND PAYS THE AUTHOR ROYALTIES FOR THE RIGHT TO PUBLISH THEIR BOOK.

However, in recent times, there has been a rise in alternative publishing models, especially self-publishing and partnership publishing. Self-publishing is publishing paid for entirely by the author and can occur in two ways. The first is where the author personally organises all the various aspects of production, from editing and design to file creation, printing, promotion and distribution. The other is where the author contracts a publishing services firm to take on the work of producing the book. Publishing services firms work with freelance editors, designers, file creators, etc., and some also offer printing and distribution services. In both cases, the author is the publisher. Self-publishing, by whatever method, can work well for authors, but it is expensive and time-consuming. Promotion and marketing are not easy, either. If you are considering self-publishing, make sure you understand the costs and production components involved. Always work with professional editors, designers and file creators, whether directly or through a publishing services firm.

Partnership publishing occurs when, in return for higher royalties, authors will contribute to some of the costs of book production, with the publisher taking on the rest of the costs. Partnership publishing is a kind of halfway house between outright self-publishing and traditional publishing. Books are professionally produced and published under the imprint of the publisher concerned, not the author.

Reputable partnership publishing should be distinguished from so-called 'vanity press publishers' who require substantial upfront payments for all costs without proper distribution or marketing. If you are considering entering into a partnership publishing contract, do your research and ask questions about everything that's involved, so you can go into it with your eyes open. You can also get advice from organisations like the Australian Society of Authors and the Small Press Network. For example, partnership publishers who wish to be members of publisher associations such as the Small Press Network in Australia, the Independent Book Publishers' Association in the US and Independent Publishers' Guild in the UK, abide by certain criteria to distinguish them from vanity publishers.

These include publishing to a high professional standard, vetting submissions (not just accepting anything sent to them), demonstrating adequate sales and providing appropriate distribution and promotion. Authors must also be paid a higher than standard royalty, to compensate them for the fact that in this model they must make a financial contribution to the book's production.

Jodie Herden and Mel Armstrong are both proud Gomeroi women. Their grandmothers were sisters, born Ella and Mei Kim. The ongoing connection with these names through their new publishing enterprise, Ella and Mei Productions, reminds them of the blessings from this beautiful culture, why they have a voice and where their strength to share comes from.

Our purpose is to provoke thought because without it, there can be no change. Bringing awareness to our similarities, irrespective of culture, plays a vital role in bridging differences. It's been such a pleasure to write so honestly of experiential ways to support more self-awareness and self-compassion for our younger generations. Following a negative experience with a partnership publisher, we investigated other ways to tell our story. We were blessed to connect with an experienced person in the field who provided wonderful practical guidance about starting the journey towards self-publishing our book, *Star Dreaming*. Moving through this experience has been positive, joyous and happy. To see the evolution of the project coming to life has been enjoyable, building excitement with every step, even when we needed to make amendments. Our focus has been on the project – creating a quality product that is beautiful, resourceful and supports learning while stimulating the hearts, minds and souls of the reader.

STAYING INSPIRED

HAVING YOUR WORK ACCEPTED BY A PUBLISHER IS A WONDERFUL MORALE BOOST FOR A WRITER OR ILLUSTRATOR, BUT IT CAN BE HARD GETTING THERE AND NOT EASY TO MAINTAIN A CAREER, EITHER.

Although the business of writing, illustrating and publishing children's books is one of the most exciting and engrossing areas to be in, it is also challenging.

Nothing is guaranteed, even for established creators and publishing teams. For those times when you're feeling the difficulties, it's great to read some inspirational words!

Established author Kate Forsyth on the power of children's books:

I'm a big believer in books that empower children and teach them that they have the power to change their world. So, I create worlds that are full of possibilities, where curses can be broken and monsters overcome. In one of my books, my child heroes are told that if you are brave of heart, sharp of wit, strong of spirit and steadfast of purpose, there is nothing you cannot achieve. I like to believe this is true, and that my child readers carry the hope of that onwards into their lives.

Publisher Chren Byng, Harper Collins Children's Books, on childhood books:

For the longest time, I've wanted copies of the long out-of-print Jan Ormerod wordless classics, *Sunshine* and *Moonlight*. My childhood copies were lost to the storage gods, and second-hand copies are expensive and rare. Then I remembered what I do for a living, and a few months back I wrote to the lovely folk at David Higham Books and asked if there was any chance of acquiring Australian rights. As luck would have it, they were just in the process of reverting rights with the latest UK publisher and so the deal was soon done.

We asked two of Jan's collaborators to reflect on what these books had meant to them, and the Australian children's literature world. And I'm so thrilled to say that both books were re-issued in February 2022, in glorious hardback, with forewords by Margaret Wild and Freya Blackwood. The books were published just a year apart – in 1981 and 1982 – with *Sunshine* named Picture Book of the Year by CBCA and *Moonlight* shortlisted in the same category. I know so many people will be as happy as I am to hold these books in our hands again. It feels good and right.

New author Anthony Sevil on nurturing your writing:

Apart from the most identical of twins, every one of us is unique, and we all probably view the world a little bit differently. I think the secret to rewarding writing is to find your uniqueness and have the confidence to honestly express those observations, thoughts and feelings. That's the necessary essence of any type of writing. A creative writing course can be beneficial to better understand the discipline and to gain confidence in your expression. Most importantly, if you have that strong desire to write, stick with it. It can be frustrating, and there are days when nothing works, but when it flows, it is a most exciting and rewarding creative pursuit.

And from professional readers – the reviewers:

Be careful around words. Words can elucidate, they can soar, comfort and heal. At their best, they lift us up. At their worst, they hurt and divide. **— Rayma Turton, editor, *Magpies* Magazine**

I review widely, across all genres and age groups. I spend a fair bit of time critiquing literary fiction, which sometimes can be turgid and excessively flowery in language. For me, turning to picture books and middle-grade fiction can offer release and relief. I think authors of these art forms should be commended for clarity, for propulsive narratives and eye-resting white spaces. **— Thuy On, reviews editor of ArtsHub**

AUTHORS, ILLUSTRATORS AND PUBLISHERS

THE CREATOR–PUBLISHER RELATIONSHIP IS A VERY SPECIAL AND UNUSUAL ONE. IT INVOLVES MUCH EMOTION AS WELL AS PRACTICAL ASPECTS

Writers and illustrators pour their heart and soul into their creations, and thus it is deeply personal. But publishers invest considerable energy, time and money in bringing that creative work to its full potential: yes, it's a business but a relational one. In the case of small publishers, especially those with a very small team, it can literally be personal, with the initial capital for the business, and thus funding for producing books, coming out of the founding partners' savings. In some cases, as with Little Pink Dog Books and Christmas Press, the publishers have worked as creators themselves, so have experienced both sides of the fence.

But although it's a personal relationship, it's also firmly professional, with frameworks of contracts, deadlines and other legal and financial aspects. Striking the right balance between the two is not always easy, and problems and hurt feelings sometimes arise. But if the foundation of a creator–publisher relationship is mutual respect, which has at its core a recognition of the rights and responsibilities on both sides, then it will be a relationship that works productively and happily for both parties.

So what's the best way, as a creator, whether writer or illustrator, to make sure that mutual respect is established between you and your publisher?

BASIC TIPS

- Remember you have both rights and responsibilities – don't assume the rights and responsibilities are all on one side, whether yours or the publishers.
- Do your due diligence with homework about the publisher, but don't approach it in an adversarial fashion.
- Look carefully at the contract and get advice on it if you want to, but don't assume that you can change every single thing or bombard the publisher with endless tweaks to it. And once you have signed an acceptable contract, make sure you abide by it (this applies to the publisher too of course!).
- Work with the suggestions that an editor makes for your manuscript. While you don't need to accept every revision, remember that editors are there to bring out the best in your book.
- Inform yourself about the different stages of your book, but don't harass publishing staff about it or try to micro-manage aspects within the publisher's control (such as design).
- Act courteously at all times, even when an issue crops up. If a disagreement does arise, it can usually be resolved in a mutually satisfactory manner if approached in the right way.

WORKING TOGETHER

In the case of picture books that are not by authorstrators, there's a third party involved, of course: your co-creator (whether writer or illustrator). It is important also to maintain good relationships with them, as well as your joint publisher. Very often, of course, the writer and illustrator will not meet in person, at least at the beginning; it is the publisher who selects the illustrator once they acquire a picture book text by a writer. To get the best possible result from that triangular relationship:

SOME MORE TIPS

- If you're a writer, respect the work of your co-creator: don't impose a rigid framework of descriptions of desired images on an illustrator. If you're an illustrator, don't impose a completely different interpretation of the text to what the writer intended – unless the writer (and the publisher) are happy for you to do that!
- It's a good idea if you'd like to be in direct correspondence with your co-creator to wait until you're at the stage when samples or storyboards have been seen and approved. Then you can either ask your publisher to put you in touch or contact your co-creator on social media – if they have public social media pages, such as author pages on Facebook or illustrator galleries on Instagram. Website contact addresses can also be a way of reaching them.
- If you do get in direct touch, and jointly decide you'd like to do some publicity for your book together, inform your publisher as they are usually very happy to help facilitate that.
- Whether you are a writer or an illustrator, always talk about 'our book' or 'my book with ...' not just 'my book' in any public announcement, post or publicity of any sort. This is a work of co-creation, and that should always be acknowledged. And while we're on this, it's a nice touch to reference the work of the designer, who is such an important part of the look of any picture book.
- Remember to acknowledge the publisher and the editor too, of course!

USEFUL ORGANISATIONS AND RESOURCES

For writers and illustrators:

The Australian Society of Authors (ASA) https://www.asauthors.org/ is the peak Australian body for both writers and illustrators. You can join as a full member (published) or associate member (unpublished). The ASA runs excellent courses, lobbies for writers and illustrators, and it has achieved many important things for all literary creators, such as Lending Rights and establishing the Copyright Agency. It can also provide contract advice and recommends rates of pay for public appearances, among other services. And for illustrators, there's the fabulous ASA Style File platform https://asastylefile.com/ where illustrators' work is showcased; it is used a lot by publishers looking for illustrators.

The Society of Children's Book Writers and Illustrators (SCBWI) is a fantastic organisation for children's writers and illustrators, offering professional development, networking, promotion and much more for its members. SCBWI is an international organisation, headquartered in the US, but with chapters all over the world. In Australia and New Zealand, we have two chapters: SCBWI Australia East and New Zealand https://australiaeastnz.scbwi.org/ and Australia West https://australiawest.scbwi.org/.

The Children's Book Council of Australia (CBCA) https://cbca.org.au/ was first established in 1945, to showcase Australian children's books, authors and publishers, and that remains its focus. It has branches in each state, and several have sub-branches in different areas. You join in your particular state. CBCA holds the prestigious Book of the Year Awards every year and biennial conferences, and state branches hold events.

Varuna, the National Writers' House, https://www.varuna.com.au/about is set in the beautiful Blue Mountains of NSW and offers residencies, classes, events and other opportunities for writers from anywhere in Australia, in any genre.

Pinerolo, the Children's Book Cottage, https://www.pinerolo.com.au/ is also set in the Blue Mountains and offers short courses, exhibitions and more.

Books Illustrated https://www.booksillustrated.com.au/ is located in Melbourne and celebrates Australian children's books illustration and illustrators. It features a showroom, exhibitions and a fantastic online shop where you can buy original artwork, prints, books and more.

Writers' Centres are for both writers and illustrators and are found in every state and territory. They offer courses, events, opportunities, networking and more, with members' discounts on these. You can find them simply by entering the name of your state or territory and 'writers' centre'. In NSW, there are also regional writers' centres, including our collaborator, the New England Writers' Centre (NEWC) www.newc.org.au. NEWC offers membership to people in our region and those further afield, as many of their courses are now online (as is the case with many writers' centres today).

The Alliance of Independent Authors https://www.allianceindependentauthors.org/ is an international organisation for self-publishing authors. Headquartered in the US, it also has ambassadors in Australia and New Zealand (among other countries).

The National Centre for Australian Children's Literature, https://www.ncacl.org.au/ is based at the University of Canberra. The NCAL is a research centre focused on children's books, housing extraordinary collections of books, MS, artwork and more. It also runs special events, advocates for children's books, and ensures that the national heritage of Australian children's books is publicly available and shared with future generations. Writers, illustrators and publishers can donate books and other material to the centre, and you can also visit on appointment to do research or view the collections.

For editors:

The Institute of Professional Editors (IPEd) http://iped-editors.org/ offers short courses and other professional development opportunities for its members and features lists of professional editor members who are available for working with both traditional publishers and self-publishers.

The Freelance Editors' Network https://www.fen.net.au/ showcases members who are available for freelance editorial work.

For designers:

Australian Book Designers' Association (ABDA) https://abda.com.au/ showcases and supports Australian book designers and offers workshops, talks and network opportunities as well as running the prestigious annual Australian Book Design Awards.

For publishers:

The Small Press Network (SPN) https://smallpressnetwork.com.au/ is the peak body for small independent publishers in Australia. It offers associate membership for self-publishers and publishing services companies. SPN runs an excellent conference every year, provides member benefits for a range of promotion services and other opportunities, and lobbies for small publishers.

The Australian Publishers' Association (APA) https://www.publishers.asn.au/ is the peak body for publishers generally in Australia. It offers short courses, workshops and other professional development opportunities, a range of member services and discounts, and lobbies for publishers.

For everyone, three essential publications:

Books+Publishing (digital only) https://www.booksandpublishing.com.au/ is the industry news digest, information source and review magazine, published every weekday and read right across the book trade and literary community.

Magpies Magazine (print only) https://www.magpies.net.au/ is the only children's books review print magazine in Australia and New Zealand, packed with great reviews and interviews and read right across the book trade and literary community. There are five issues a year.

Good Reading Magazine (print and digital) https://www.goodreadingmagazine.com.au/ is an excellent colour magazine dedicated to book reviews, including children's books, aimed at the general reader and libraries. There are 11 issues a year. *Good Reading* also publishes two digital magazines aimed at young readers, parents and teachers: *PK Mag* (for primary school age) and *SpineOut* (for secondary school age).

A small selection of Australian online newsletters, ezines and review sites for children's books:

Buzz Words (subscription, fortnightly) http://www.buzzwordsmagazine.com/p/about-buzz-words.html

Pass It On (subscription, weekly) https://jackiehoskingpio.wordpress.com/

Reading Time (free reviews site run by CBCA) https://cbca.org.au/reading-time

Read Plus (subscription reviews site) https://www.readplus.com.au/

Kids' Book Review (free reviews and interviews site) http://www.kids-bookreview.com

ACKNOWLEDGEMENTS

The world is a brighter place, thanks to people who write, illustrate and produce children's books.

Initiated by the New England Writers' Centre with the generous support of Create NSW, this book has been created by United Publishers of Armidale, as a genuinely exciting team effort. Thanks to everyone on the *Inside Story* writing team, Sophie Masson, Kathy Creamer, Beattie Alvarez and Peter Creamer, for sharing your combined expertise and experiences in the wonderful world of writing, illustrating and publishing children's books. Thanks also to our thoughtful editors, Jen Scanlan and Sharnee Rawson, and our very creative designer, Rae Ainsworth.

Many thanks to the following individual people – writers, illustrators, editors, designers, agents and publishers from all over Australia – who generously contributed fabulous quotes, advice, tips and images:

Alexandra Adsett, Rae Ainsworth, Beattie Alvarez, David Allan, Mel Armstrong, Stephen Axelsen, Duncan Ball, Dianne Bates, Sami Bayly, Anna Bell, Tash Besliev, Rachel Bin Salleh, Jenny Blackford, Janeen Brian, Chren Byng, Amy Calautti, Lorena Carrington, Paul Collins, Margaret Connolly, Heidi Cooper Smith, Meredith Costain, Kathy Creamer, Peter Creamer, Anthony Davis, Kristin Devine, Katrin Dreiling, Ursula Dubosarsky, Kate Durack, Hazel Edwards, Katrina Fisher, Mandy Foot, Kate Forsyth, Rebecca Fung, Susanne Gervay, Lesley Gibbes, Libby Gleeson, Amy Golbach, Nicki Greenberg, Jenny Hale, Simone Hale, Demelsa Haughton, John Heffernan, Jodie Herden, Simon Higgins, Jackie Hosking, Simon Howe, Fiona Inglis, Ian Irvine, George Ivanoff, Ann James, Dmetri Kakmi, Ingrid Kallick, Jan Latta, Cathi Lewis, Lorraine Marwood, Pippa Masson, Sophie Masson, Phoebe McArthur, Rachael McDiarmid, Fiona McDonald, Lesley McGee, Brenton E McKenna, Eva Mills, Thuy On, Cheryl Orsini, Sue Pillans, Vicky Pratt, Natalie Jane Prior, Michael Pryor, Sharnee Rawson, Sally Rippin, Judith Rossell, Jen Scanlan, Sandra Severgnini, Anthony Sevil, Stephanie Smee, Craig Smith, Anne Spudvilas, Lisa Stewart, Shaun Tan, Richard Tulloch, Rayma Turton, Gabrielle Wang, Jenny (Yuxiao) Wang, Patricia Ward, Ruth Waters, Laura Wood and Michelle Worthington.

Many thanks also to the many people who backed our crowdfunding campaign. We really appreciate it!

Thanks go in particular to the following people:

Lyndal Knuckey, Xavier Masson-Leach, Karel Vine, Louis-Xavier and Francia Masson, Sandra van Doorn, Claudine Tinellis, Olivier Masson, Clifford & Megan Ainsworth, Lorena Carrington and Lizzie Horne.

PERMISSIONS FROM PUBLISHERS

WITH THANKS TO THE FOLLOWING PUBLISHERS FOR PERMISSION TO USE IMAGES FROM THEIR TITLES:

Book Trail Press for images from *The March of the Ants* (Ursula Dubosarsky/Tohby Riddle, 2021) 2
Dirt Lane Press for image from *The Snowman's Wish* (Sophie Masson/Ronak Taher, 2020) 2
Affirm Press for image from *The Very Noisy Baby* (Alison Lester, 2017) 5
Hachette Australia for images from *The Lost Thing* (Shaun Tan, 2000) 10
ABC Books/Harper Collins for images from *The Secret Army* (Sophie Masson/Anthony Davis, 2006) 11
Magabala Books for images and cover from *Ubby's Underdogs: The Legend of the Phoenix Dragon* (Brenton E McKenna, 2011) 11
Magabala Books for cover image from *Deadly D and Justice Jones: Making the Team* (Scott Prince/Dave Hartley, 2013) 16
HarperCollins for images from *Withering-by-Sea* (Judith Rossell, 2014) 17
Magabala Books for cover image from *Black Cockatoo* (Carl Merrison/Hakea Hustle, 2018) 19
Affirm Press for cover image from *The Detective's Guide to Ocean Travel* (Nicky Greenberg, 2020) 20
Magabala Books for cover image from *Our Birds: Ŋilimurruŋgu Wäyin Malanynha* (Siena Stubbs, 2018) 22
True To Life Books for cover image from *Chipper, the Cheetah* (Jan Latta, 2003) 22
Wild Dingo Press for cover image from *STEM Stars: Gisela Kaplan* (Emily Gale, 2021) 24
HarperCollins for images for 'Counting Chicks/Comptine des Poussins' (Sophie Masson/Lisa Stewart) from *A Boat of Stars* (ed. Margaret Connolly/Natalie Jane Prior, 2018) 26
Scholastic Australia for cover image from *On My Way* by Sophie Masson and Simon Howe Text copyright © Sophie Masson, 2019. Illustrations copyright © Simon Howe, 2019. First published by Scholastic Press, a division of Scholastic Australia Pty Limited, 2019. Reproduced with permission from Scholastic Australia Pty Limited. 32
Affirm Press for cover image from *The Very Noisy Baby* (Alison Lester, 2018) 32
Hachette Australia for cover image from *The Arrival* (Shaun Tan, 2006) 32
Ella and Mei Productions for cover image from *Star Dreaming* (Jodie Herden/Mel Armstrong, 2022) 33
Dirt Lane Press for cover image from *The Snowman's Wish* (Sophie Masson/Ronak Taher, 2020) 33
Book Trail Press for cover image from *The March of the Ants* (Ursula Dubosarsky/Tohby Riddle, 2021) 33
EK Books for cover image from *At the End of Holyrood Lane* (Dimity Powell/Nicky Johnston) 33
Magabala Books for cover image from *Mad Magpie*, (Gregg Dreise, 2016) 33
EK Books for images from *At the End of Holyrood Lane* (Dimity Powell/Nicky Johnston, 2018) 36
Scholastic Australia images from *On My Way* by Sophie Masson and Simon Howe. Text copyright © Sophie Masson, 2019. Illustrations copyright © Simon Howe, 2019. First published by Scholastic Press, a division of Scholastic Australia Pty Limited. 39, 47
Allen & Unwin for images from *Swan Lake* (Anne Spudvilas, 2017) 52
Lothian/Hachette for images from *Joey and Riley* (Mandy Foot, 2019) 53
Hachette Australia for images from *The Arrival* (Shaun Tan, 2006) 60

PERMISSIONS FROM PUBLISHERS

CONTINUED

UNITED PUBLISHERS OF ARMIDALE IMAGE INDEX

FEATURED IMAGES FROM CHRISTMAS PRESS AND LITTLE PINK DOG BOOKS.

PICTURE BOOKS (LITTLE PINK DOG BOOKS)

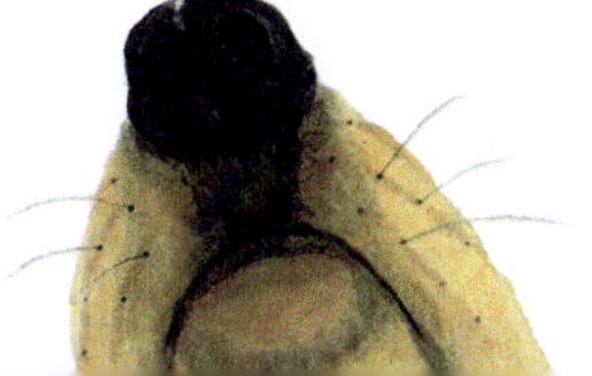

ILLUSTRATED STORYBOOKS & FICTION ANTHOLOGIES (CHRISTMAS PRESS)

CHAPTER BOOKS, JUNIOR FICTION AND MIDDLE-GRADE FICTION (CHRISTMAS PRESS)

PLEASE NOTE THAT EAGLE BOOKS IS AN IMPRINT OF CHRISTMAS PRESS.

POETRY AND VERSE NOVELS (CHRISTMAS PRESS)

PLAYS (CHRISTMAS PRESS)

MEET THE INSIDE STORY TEAM

Born in Indonesia of French parents, who are themselves of mixed ethnicity – Basque, Spanish, Portuguese, French-Canadian as well as French – and brought up in France and Australia, Sophie Masson is the award-winning and internationally published author of over 70 books for children, young adults and adults. Her fiction for children ranges widely over genres and age groups, including historical, mystery, thriller, fantasy, chapter books, middle-grade, illustrated storybooks and picture books. Her short stories, poetry and non-fiction have also been published. The holder of a PhD from the University of New England, Sophie is co-director of Armidale-based publisher Christmas Press, Chair of the New England Writers' Centre, and President of the Small Press Network. In 2019, Sophie received an AM in the Order of Australia for significant service to literature as an author and publisher, and for her work in literary organisations.

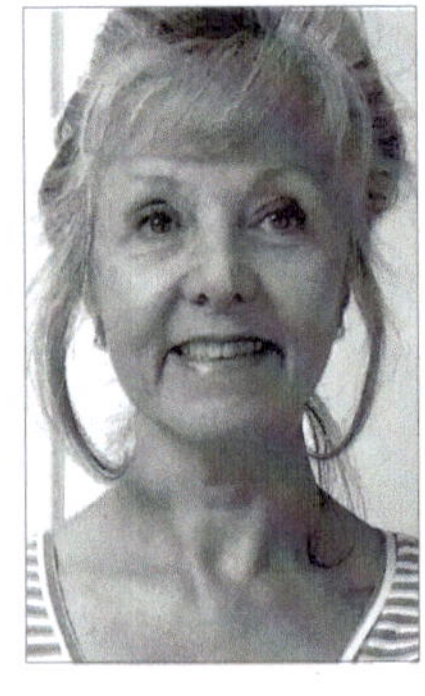

Kathy Creamer is an award-winning writer and illustrator who has been published by Oxford University Press, Reed International, Christmas Press, Williamstown Literary Festival and many other organisations. She has a Bachelor of Arts Honours Degree in Creative Writing and Children's Literature, and a Master of Arts Degree in Children's Book Illustration from the renowned Cambridge School of Art in England. She has also run her own successful publishing venture, which was based in the UK. Having recently moved to Armidale with her husband, Peter, she has set up Little Pink Dog Books Children's Publishing to help new and emerging writers and illustrators to enter the children's picture book market.

Beattie Alvarez is a tyrannical commissioning editor. She is tough. She is addicted to coffee. She is generally cranky. In her spare time, she is an author, designer and dragon hatcher. She has several books with her name on the cover, a few anthologies with her name on a story inside, and permanent scars from the dragon hatching (there's also the editing she does, the shop she runs and the illustrations she occasionally draws).

Peter Creamer is a doctoral qualified mechanical engineer who trained at Rolls Royce. Over 35 years, he worked in power generation for several multinational companies. With a change of sector, he now works as the Chief Operating Officer at the University of New England in Australia. After he and Kathy met and had children, they developed a joint love of children's picture books. With Kathy's expertise in the writing and illustrating of children's books, it was only natural that they started producing children's picture books. Their first venture produced 20 books for the UK market. Upon moving to Australia, they formed Little Pink Dog Books to help provide opportunities for new and emerging children's authors and illustrators.
To date, they have published over 35 books that have won many awards. Peter concentrates on the marketing, promotion and production of children's books for Little Pink Dog Books.

Jen Scanlan is a professional editor and member of the Institute of Professional Editors. She studied Education and Visual Arts at WSU. She later completed two courses, with Newcastle University and Capstone Editing, to become a qualified editor, proofreader and copywriter. Since moving to Armidale in 2020, she has connected with the wonderful world of children's books, editing picture books to young adult fiction. Jen also edits academic and educational texts. Her freelance business, Heights Proofreading, provides a full range of editing services, as well as other related services such as copywriting and preparing educational materials. In one of Jen's former occupations as a teacher of English and Visual Arts, she developed her ethos of 'creativity, communication, cats and chocolate'.

Sharnee Rawson is a recent graduate of the University of New England. She earned her bachelor degree in media and communications and completed a Bachelor of Media and Communications with Honours in 2021. Throughout her studies, Sharnee worked at the regional News Corp publication *The Daily Examiner* and the online news platform *Tune!FM*.
While working as an intern at Christmas Press, she edited the junior fiction book *Fil and Harry* (by Jenny Blackford). She continues to pursue a budding career in the publishing industry with a particular interest in books for children and young adults.

Rae Ainsworth is creative by nature, and a designer by nurture. She says, 'I love layout. I find it foundational. Good layout draws your eye to smoothly survey the content hierarchy. Its dynamic tension gets you involved in the dialogue between content types ... and I feel that it can "lift the stage" so that all the elements almost feel alive and moving. I love working with illustrators, writers and publishers. It's an honour. Bringing out the best in good people and in great work empowers my work. And work made for children enlivens my drive to challenge the world.'

The more that you read, the more things you will know.
The more that you learn, the more places you'll go. — **Dr Seuss, *I Can Read With My Eyes Shut***

Cover illustration credits

Front cover: Patricia Ward, Kathy Creamer, Fiona McDonald, Amy Golbach

Back cover: David Allan, Jenny Hale, Dr Suzie Starfish, Shaun Tan, Lesley Gibbes, Kathy Creamer, Phoebe McArthur, Lesley McGee

UPA Books logo: illustration by Kristin Devine, design by Rae Ainsworth

Christmas
Press